ZZZZZAPPED

and other encouraging words

BOB AND JUDY NEUMAN

ZZZZZAPPED **and other encouraging words.** Copyright © Bob and Judy Neuman. All rights reserved. No part of this book shall be reproduced or transmitted in any form or by any means, without the exception of brief, credited quotations, without prior written permission by the authors.

CONTACT US AT:

StalledVW@aol.com

ISBN 979-8-223-4750-1

DEDICATION:

"To the glory of God!"

TABLE OF CONTENTS

PREFACE:

In the Beginning!
Bob Neuman

On March 22, 1999, Judy and I published the first edition of a periodic newsletter we called *"An encouraging word . . ."* and sub-titled it, *"The letter ministry of Pastor Bob and Judy Neuman."*

At that time I felt the need to communicate with Alice, a friend of ours, some words of encouragement on a regular basis. She was suffering from "agoraphobia," a type of anxiety disorder, which means "fear of place, assembly, or marketplace."

Alice chose to be "cooped up" in her own home until her husband, George, began attending the church I pastored. Eventually, Alice joined him and became less fearful and more trusting.

Judy and I took turns writing the newsletter and, on many occasions, we co-wrote them. In the newsletters we shared our own adventures and experiences, and believe that God was leading us in this ministry.

We printed copies and distributed them. In addition, I sent them out via e-mail, as well as posting them on my Facebook page.

We gave them to servers at restaurants, to nurses in the doctor's office, and to many other people with whom we had contact.

Over the course of time, we were "encouraged" by several acquaintances to compile the newsletter in book form. This is that endeavor, and represents just a portion of the articles we wrote.

Unless otherwise indicated, all Scripture references are from *The New International Version of the Bible.*

Our first newsletter was titled "Pancakes . . . or Chicken?" and, because of that, it has the lead-off position in this compilation.

Each newsletter ended with a section which we titled "On the Lighter Side." This original essay follows that tradition, but the others in this book are given under "Bob's Final Thoughts." On a few occasions, the "Final Thoughts" are shared by Judy.

It is our prayer that you will be encouraged, entertained, and blessed by this book.

CHAPTER ONE

PANCAKES . . . OR CHICKEN?

Bob Neuman

A five-year-old said grace at the family dinner one night. "Dear God," he prayed, "thank you for these pancakes."

When he concluded, his parents asked him why he thanked God for pancakes when they were having chicken.

He smiled and said, "I thought I would see if God was paying attention tonight."

When we go through difficulties in our lives, and face circumstances that seem insurmountable, we often wonder: (1) Is God there? and (2) Is He "paying attention?"

Many years ago, the Lord gave Judy a beautiful song which is a favorite of mine. I'd like to share it with you.

JESUS CARES!

Verse 1:

> There is One who cares about your problems,
>
> One who stands by you.
>
> He will lift the load you carry
>
> when you don't know what to do.

Jesus Christ can make you whole,

just place your life in His control.

Then His presence will go with you everywhere.

Chorus:

Jesus cares about your problems, yes, He cares!

Jesus understands each heartache (He's been there!)

He'll never leave you,

He'll never walk away when you're in need.

Jesus bears your heavy burden for He cares!

Verse 2:

He's your Rock of strength, a Hiding Place,

real comfort when you're blue.

In the midst of fear

those everlasting arms are holding you.

Cast your worries upon Jesus;

rest in Him because He cares.

He has promised that He always will be there!

© 1983 Judith Crane Neuman

A number of you who are reading this letter are going through times of discouragement. But I want to assure you that Jesus cares . . . and we do, too!

He is there . . . and He is paying attention! Jesus said, *"I am with you always, even to the end of the age"* (Matthew 28:20).

The writer to the Hebrew Christians agreed when he wrote, ". . . *for He Himself* [Jesus] *said, 'I will never desert you, nor will I ever forsake you'. . . 'Jesus Christ is the same yesterday and today, and forever'."* (Hebrews 13:5, 8).

ON THE LIGHTER SIDE

In 1999, Judy and I underwent a cardiac health screening at Ingalls Hospital in Harvey, Illinois..

For $39.00 each, we received an electrocardiogram, blood work, monitored exercise, and a body-fat analysis.

A few days later, we each received a large envelope in which several pages detailed how we did on the various tests, analyzed our overall health, and made recommendations.

The tests revealed that Judy and I shared two of the same health-risk factors: (1) Our age—hello! We can't help that, and (2) Our weight. Obviously, this part of our newsletter—"On The Lighter Side"—has nothing to do with our weight. And, I feel I should mention that when I step on a talking scale, it does *not* say, "One person at a time, please."

After we re-read the health reports, I said to Judy, "So we just paid $78.00 to have these experts tell us that we're old and fat?"

CHAPTER TWO

"ALL GOD'S CHILDREN GOT SHOES!"

Judy Neuman

"Mommy, I don't have any boots that fit me, and there's a snowstorm coming." Eight-year-old Natalie's voice quivered as she tried to hold back the tears. The weatherman had predicted deep snow that week, and our daughter, Natalie, and our five-year-old daughter, Lori, had to walk four blocks to school every day.

I was also concerned about the "boots" dilemma, but I knew that we didn't have the extra money to buy them that week.

Standing in front of the kitchen sink, I wrapped my arms around Natalie and said, "Let's pray about those boots!" I began to pray a simple prayer, asking God to provide boots before the snowstorm arrived. Then I kissed the children and sent them off to school.

With a busy day before me, I soon forgot about our morning prayer, that is, until I brought the mail inside the house that afternoon. As I sorted through the junk mail, my eyes spotted an envelope from a friend of ours who served as pastor of another Assemblies of God church in a nearby suburb of Chicago.

Inside the envelope was a nice note thanking Bob for speaking at his church a few weeks earlier. Much to my surprise a check was enclosed. Bob had not expected to receive an honorarium, but God knew way ahead of time that a little girl named, Natalie, would need a new pair of boots before a snowstorm arrived.

"I SAY A LITTLE PRAYER FOR YOU!"

Prayer was never a stranger in our home. Bob and I always prayed with our children at mealtime and at bedtime. And I even prayed for them before they were born that they would grow up to be what God wanted them to be. While they were still babies, I prayed for their future husbands, and for the parents who were raising them.

However, at times I would slack off in my prayers for Natalie and Lori, especially if everything seemed to be going well.

But God got my attention at one of our monthly ministers' wives' meetings several years ago. We were discussing prayer, and one of the ladies asked, "If we mothers don't pray for our children, WHO WILL?" That statement made me think! At that point, daily prayers for my kids became a greater priority.

I've approached God in prayer as a happy mom, a sad one, and a mad one. I have cried out to God on their behalf concerning their health, their safety, and their friends.

But my most consistent prayer has been for their spiritual health—the most important prayer a mother can pray, one that can have an eternal effect upon their lives as they nurture an intimate relationship with the living God.

THANKFUL FOR A GODLY HERITAGE

I often offer thanks to the Lord for my parents, Pete and Theresa Crane. They not only loved us by providing all of the practical things my brother, Steve, and I needed, such as housing, food, clothing, and schooling, but also cared about our spiritual development. They were God-fearing, church-going people of integrity who set a wonderful example for us. In addition to that, they loved us enough to pray for us.

WHAT AN INSPIRATION!

My grandmother, Meda Jolliff, who always called herself "Old Granny Jolliff," was especially gifted in the ministry of prayer. She taught a ladies' Bible study at her church for many years, and spent much time in prayer for, and with, the women in her class.

Even when her age and health limited her church attendance, some of the women from the church, as well as her neighbors, would call, or drop by her home to ask her to pray with them.

Most importantly, she prayed for her own two children, her three grandchildren (one of whom was me), and the three great-grandchildren that she loved so much. She helped to pray me through the teenage years, marriage, and the birth of our two children.

She prayed for us as we raised our kids, and she prayed for Natalie as we brought her to Missouri to enroll in college, as well as for Lori when she graduated from eighth grade.

GRANNY'S LEGACY

Our last visit with "Old Granny Jolliff" was on Mother's Day, 1986. Two months later she died at the age of 89 resting peacefully in her recliner at her tiny home in Springfield, Missouri.

She didn't have many possessions to leave to her family, but her loving prayers for us are a legacy that we will always treasure!

After Granny's death in 1986, Mom's homegoing in 1995, and Dad's passing in 2000, it suddenly dawned upon me that they have passed the baton of prayer to my generation. As the oldest one left of my original family, I feel even more responsible and privileged to be a prayer warrior on behalf of my family, as well as others God chooses to send across my pathway.

A MOTHER'S MIRACULOUS PRAYER

I heard a true story that happened during the Soviet occupation of Romania. Thousands of Christians had been deported to Siberia, one of whom was a woman named Lydia.

During the daytime she was assigned the duty of chopping down trees in the forest. All prisoners were kept in small cells, and fed only a bowl of soup after the workday was over. Each one was responsible to cut down a certain number of trees per day or they would be beaten, and go unfed. One day, other prisoners stole Lydia's wood, and she didn't meet the quota!

That evening her food was withheld. Sad, hungry and sleepless she took a walk into the prison yard as she wept prayerfully.

Suddenly a prison guard yelled out, "Hey! Do you have a mother?" (She did have an elderly Christian mother back in Romania.)

"For one half hour I've been following you, trying to shoot you with my revolver, but I can't move my arm. . . . It is surely your mother who prays for you!"

Lydia ran back to her cell, where she slept like a baby, sensing the protection of the Lord.

The next day, her work area was surrounded by many guards and dogs. Though not allowed to speak to the prisoners, the guard she had met the night before caught her eye. Then he raised his arm to show her that today his arm was all right!

An atheistic guard saw God's miraculous intervention, and Lydia's life was spared—all because her mother prayed.

BOB'S FINAL THOUGHTS

Testimonies abound of people who have experienced God's providential deliverance at just the right time.

Such incidents have even been confirmed when a person checks, asking, "Exactly when were you praying for me?"

CHAPTER THREE

AN ALARMING EXPERIENCE
Bob and Judy Neuman

"Diddles is sick, and may be on his way out," Judy said, with a concerned look on her face as she hung up the telephone.

In 2012 Diddles was the cat owned by Ruth, our 79-year-old widowed friend from Lansing, Illinois. She had called to ask if Judy could take her and Diddles to a veterinarian because her relatives were at work.

Judy took them to Dr. Matthews, our own vet, who examined Diddles and said he would need to keep him for a few days. The cat was dehydrated, and several tests would be required to determine the problem.

We stopped by Ruth's home early the next morning to give her the name and phone number of the veterinarian so that she and her son would be able to retrieve Diddles a few days later.

Ruth turned on her porch light, saw that it was us, and opened the door.

We barely entered her home when her telephone rang. In addition to that, we heard a funny beeping sound coming from her hallway. She excused herself as she went towards her bedroom as the phone rang. Soon she returned, picked up the phone, and said, "It's okay. I was the one who opened the door."

She saw the puzzled looks on our faces, and informed us that she had forgotten to turn off her ADT alarm system when she welcomed us at the door. Next, she warned us that the police would be arriving soon.

The words barely left her lips when she noticed flashing lights in her driveway, and remarked, "I think they're here."

Feeling a little like criminals, Judy and I accompanied Ruth to the door, and she said to the policeman, "It's okay. This is Pastor Bob and Judy."

I explained to the officer who we were, and why we were there. As I did so, a second squad car arrived. The first officer waved him off, indicating that everything was fine. This was the only time I ever had to convince an officer of the law that Judy had been guilty of being a cat chauffeur, not a cat burglar!

Sad to say, Diddles spent the night at the veterinarian's office, but passed away the next day, despite all of the veterinarian's valiant efforts. But, thankfully, Judy and I spent the night in our own beds instead of on cots in a jail cell!

AIRPORT INSECURITY

Judy and I experienced a different type of incident involving an alarm system several years ago when our oldest daughter, Natalie, was flying back to college in Missouri after the holidays.

The story you are about to read is true. It happened at Midway Airport in Chicago long before the al-Qaeda terrorist attacks in 2001. In those days, people could accompany their family and friends all the way to the boarding area and visit with them until they boarded the plane.

Natalie was going through her "punk stage." At the time, I wished that it had been a "stage"-coach, and that she was heading out of town on it! I guess Southwest Airlines offered a smoother ride.

There she stood, sporting a Mohawk haircut, ragged shorts, a large chain around her neck, and makeshift paper-clip earrings dangling from an ear, with a pair of children's scissors attached. We wish we had photographed her that day for the Neuman archives!

Natalie breezed right through the security checkpoint, in spite of her metallic ornaments!

Now picture me. As a conservatively dressed, mild-mannered man with no metal attached to, or dangling from, any part of my body, I had to be the epitome of a non-terrorist.

I walked through the gateway only to hear the alarm sound. The guard ordered me to go back and take everything out of my pockets. So I placed the pens I had in my shirt pocket in the tray, along with my wristwatch. I strode confidently through the gateway again. Yes, for the second time I heard the alarm.

I looked up to see two of Chicago's finest "men in blue" with suspicion written all over their faces! Then the guard motioned for another security employee to join him.

As he waved the wand over me, I noticed Judy standing off to the side with a dreamy look in her eyes. I suspected that she was hoping the wand-waving officer would be able to change me into a handsome prince! Unfortunately, that didn't happen.

My Achilles heel seemed to be the magnetic strips on the credit cards I had in my billfold. After I removed my wallet, I finally received the airport's unofficial Seal of Approval. To this day, I do not think it was the magnetic strips on those cards that caused the trouble. I believe it was my magnetic personality!

CAUGHT "RED-HANDED"
Judy Neuman

Can you picture this scene? The shades were drawn, and only the light from the hall window shone into the kitchen. A small hand stretched across the counter toward a hand-painted cookie jar. The other hand grasped the lid and quietly removed it.

Grimy fingers pulled a chocolate-chip cookie from the container. (P.S. to my brother, Steve, who may have his hand in a cookie jar at this very moment: "This is a hypothetical situation and isn't really a story from our childhood.")

"Crash!" went the lid that had been placed too close to the counter's edge. A loud voice soon filled the room. "Johnny! Didn't I tell you not to eat any cookies before supper?"

This scene reminds me of what my mother might have said in such a situation: "Caught like a rat in a trap!"

Did Johnny just now learn that it was wrong to eat that cookie? Not at all. First, his mother had given him instructions, and had set down a rule. Second, as he pondered whether or not to disobey, an alarm went off inside of him—his conscience. It warned him that to eat that cookie would be wrong, and would bring the consequence of either a scolding, or some other disciplinary action.

"ALARM."
DOESN'T THAT WORD TELL US SOMETHING?

The purpose of an alarm is to protect us from possible danger, and its related consequences. Thankfully, many lives have been spared, and property protected because of alarms that detected smoke, carbon monoxide, or intruders. Sometimes, the alarm may be nothing more than a barking dog!

There is a spiritual lesson to be learned from these examples. God's built-in alarm system, our conscience, is of vital importance to us in our day-to-day living. It is one way God sounds a warning to us when we encounter situations in which we are tempted to do something illegal, immoral, or unloving.

"Sin" is God's description of such actions. There are always consequences when we ignore that alarm within us.

We've all heard stories about people who have died in fires because the smoke detector batteries had gone dead. That can happen to our spiritual alarm system, too. If we keep on ignoring our God-given conscience, it becomes deadened, and cannot properly alert us when we're tempted to sin. The Bible warns against liars *"seared in their own conscience as with a branding iron"* (1 Timothy 4:2, *The New American Standard Version).* How sad that many will face spiritual death because of a "seared," or dead conscience.

The Bible tells us that such living is not living at all.

Our alarm system is meant to pull us toward God. He wants us to be spiritually alive and well!

If you feel like your spiritual batteries are dead, you may pray a prayer similar to what King David prayed in the Bible, *"Search me, O God, and know my heart; test my thoughts. Point out anything you find in me that makes you sad, and lead me along the path to everlasting life"* (Psalm 139:23-24, *The Living Bible).*

In response to genuine prayer, God's Holy Spirit will reveal to you the sinful barricades that separate you from God. Then you'll be able to admit those sins, ask for His forgiveness, and receive His cleansing through the shed blood of Jesus Christ His Son.

In closing, we want to share an "alarming" truth with you, and may it awaken you to God's plan for your life: *"For God so loved the world that he gave his one and only Son, that whoever believes in him shall not perish but have eternal life"* (John 3:16).

BOB'S FINAL THOUGHTS

Ivan Pavlov was a Russian experimental neurologist, and psychologist. He is best known for his discovery of classical conditioning through his experiments with dogs. He trained hungry dogs to salivate at the sound of a metronome or buzzer, which was previously associated with the sight of food. Pavlov conditioned the dogs by ringing a bell before feeding them, and they salivated.

Then he eventually rang the bell, but removed the food. He discovered that the dogs still salivated, and he referred to this learned response as a "conditioned reflex."

As strange as it may seem, I acknowledge that, long after my airport security incident with Natalie, I suffered a Pavlovian response.

Judy and I were at Midway Airport in Chicago, going on a brief trip in 2002.

Before leaving our house, I emptied my pockets of all excess items. That included most of the keys I usually carry, as well as extra credit cards. Then I handed my loose change to Judy to place in her purse. I figured it would be better for her to get stopped at the security check-point than me. Judy asked me, "Is there also a Pavlov test for 'chickens'?"

As we approached the security checkpoint, I saw that my ball point pens remained in my pocket. I quickly shoved them into my briefcase just before I placed it on the conveyor belt.

This time, like Pavlov's dogs, I passed the test.

I thought about getting a T-shirt emblazoned with, "I Survived Midway Airport's Security Screening, 2002."

CHAPTER FOUR

A CASE OF MISTAKEN IDENTITY

Bob Neuman

An elderly Jewish lady was flying from New York City to Miami Beach. She looked at the young businessman sitting next to her and asked, "Excuse me, sir. Are you Jewish?"

"No, ma'am," he replied politely.

A short time later she repeated her question by stating, "You're really Jewish, aren't you?"

Once again the man assured her that he was not Jewish, and returned to reading his book.

Shortly after the plane lifted off, the woman looked him over again and asked, "Are you positive you're not Jewish?"

By now the young man was frustrated and, hoping to stop further questions by the lady, declared, "O.K., ma'am. I am Jewish."

"Funny," the lady exclaimed as she looked at him with a puzzled look on her face, "you don't look Jewish."

Have you ever been mistaken for somebody else? I have.

"'HOPE" AS IN "BOB!"

For 25 years I served as a part-time chaplain at a State of Illinois facility for individuals with developmental disabilities. Judy and I usually ministered together. She accompanied me every Friday as an unpaid volunteer to the campus that housed seven different units of 10 houses each. She brought a small keyboard, and during our two hours, we visited each house on Unit One. There we sang, interacted, and prayed with the individuals living there, as well as with the staff.

One of my other duties, which I usually did alone, was to visit individuals from the whole facility who were hospitalized locally.

William, known as "Billy," was a young man from a different unit. The first time I met him was on a hospital visit. When I entered his room, his mother was present. I introduced myself and said, "I'm Chaplain Bob," adding that I served at the facility where William lived.

When Billy heard the name, "Bob," his eyes brightened, and he said with excitement in his voice, "Bob Hope."

I do not think I look anything like Bob Hope, but I hope I brought some hope and joy into Billy's life. Every time I saw Billy after that, I was always "Bob Hope."

JUST CALL ME "PEANUT BUTTER"

Since Judy and I ministered together so much, some people referred to us as "Peanut Butter and Jelly." A number of folks simply called us "PB&J."(To many, it just meant "Pastor Bob and Judy.")

Judy and I met Dave and Pat through the ministry of The Lansing Community Pantry which was housed in the church where I served as pastor. They became very good friends, and they soon embraced us as "PB&J."

Later, Dave was diagnosed with cancer, and had been undergoing treatments. One day, we received a call from Pat saying that Dave had suffered a stroke, and had been admitted to the hospital.

Judy and I visited him. When we entered the room, Pat looked at Dave, pointed at me, and asked, "Do you know who that is? That's Pastor Bob."

My heart sank as I heard Dave emphatically utter the word, "No!" I thought perhaps his mind had been affected by the stroke. But then he quickly added, "Peanut Butter!"

I'm not quite sure how Dave saw me at the time. Because of my size, I imagine I looked like "chunky peanut butter."

A DEAD GIVEAWAY!

After Jesus was falsely accused and brought before the religious authorities of His day, Peter, one of Jesus' closest disciples, followed Him, and tried to blend in with the crowd.

As Peter warmed himself by the fire, he was accused of being a follower of Jesus. The Gospel of Matthew records what happened. *"After a little while, those standing there went up to Peter and said, 'Surely you are one of them, for your accent gives you away'"* (Matthew 26:73).

That would be followed by two other occasions when Peter would be "outed," and would eventually deny knowing Jesus.

A REAL CHRISTIAN IS "AN OPEN BOOK"

The Apostle Paul wrote these words to the church that was located in Corinth, a major city of Greece: *"You yourselves are our letter, written on our hearts, known and read by everybody. You show that you are a letter from Christ, the result of our ministry, written not with ink but with the Spirit of the living God, not on tablets of stone but on tablets of human hearts"* (2 Corinthians 3:2-3).

The early Christians were known both by what they SAID, and by what they DID.

Pliny the Younger (62-c. 113) was Governor of Bithynia, an ancient region, kingdom, and Roman province in the northwestern part of Asia Minor. Pliny was quite hostile to Christians. He wrote a letter in 106 AD to the emperor, Trajan, in which he included a report on proceedings against Christians.

In an extensive explanation to his supervisor, Pliny explained that he forced Christians to "curse Christ, which a genuine Christian cannot be induced to do." He also wrote this description of the activities and practices they followed:

"They affirmed, however, that the whole of their guilt, or their error, was that they were in the habit of meeting on a certain fixed day before it was light, when they sang in alternate verse a hymn to Christ as to a god, and bound themselves by solemn oath, not to do any wicked deeds, but never to commit any fraud, theft, adultery, never to falsify their word, not to deny a trust when they should be called upon to deliver it up."

It sounds to me as if those Christians were beautiful letters known and read by all men, including people who viewed them as their enemies.

May all of us be such living letters!

BOB'S FINAL THOUGHTS

God truly has blessed Judy and me with many friends throughout the years. Two of them were sisters, named Gladys and Mildred. They were long-time members of our church, and were very fun-loving souls.

One day, Mildred, the older of the two, was reading the paper when she spoke up and said to her sister, "Gladys, listen to this: It says 'One out of every four people in the world is Chinese'."

Then she asked, "Which one of the Neumans do you think is Chinese?"

So, who am I really? Judging from the illustrations, I trust you have reached the conclusion that I am neither Jewish . . . nor Bob Hope . . . nor a jar of peanut butter . . . nor even Chinese.

Well, then, who am I?

Perhaps I could describe myself in the words made popular by a sailor named Popeye: "I yam what I yam!"

More truthfully, I am a man who has been made in the image of God. Because of His mercy, my sins are cleansed by the blood of Jesus Christ! So you may call me a "Christian," and that is no mistake!

CHAPTER FIVE

"AND THE ANSWER IS . . ."
Judy Neuman

The category is: "Countries of the world."

The answer is: "Grape vineyards, the Acropolis, the Aegean Sea."

If your question is, "What is Greece?" you would be correct. You might even continue with correct answers, and win big money on the popular TV game show, *"Jeopardy!"*

Greece is not only the "Question" to the *Jeopardy* "Answer," but also the country that Bob and I toured for 10 days in September, 2015, to celebrate our 50th wedding anniversary. What an enjoyable, inspiring, and educational time it was.

Humorous incidents seem to stalk us at every turn, and this trip was no different, as you will see in the following accounts.

THE MYSTERIOUS DISAPPEARING TOURIST

I lost Bob during a tour of a museum in Athens, Greece. Before the tour, our busload of about 40 people had the opportunity to use the restrooms.

Bob said he would wait for me, but when I exited the restroom, he was nowhere in sight. Of course, I deduced that he had already joined the group at the elevators, so I proceeded to do the same.

However, the tour guide had not seen him either, so 39 of us took the elevators to the third floor to begin the tour—without Bob! I couldn't concentrate on the interesting displays because I kept wondering if Bob had passed out in the restroom, or had a heart attack in a remote hallway.

Finally, the tour guide stopped the whole tour, and had everyone sit down for a while until Bob was found.

A fellow tourist, Pat, and I went back downstairs to look for Bob. A museum employee had seen him go up the escalator earlier, so at least we knew he was physically okay. Pat and I went back to join our group, but there was still no Bob!

Because of this interruption of our tour, some fellow tourists were quite aggravated, while others were just happy to sit down and rest.

One sympathetic lady looked at me with a "knowing" expression on her face, and with compassion in her voice, asked, "Is he in the habit of wandering off?"

("Not yet," I thought). "No," I answered.

Finally, I asked the tour guide to continue the tour with the group. Pat and I decided to leave the museum, wait outside with the other busload of tourists in our tour, and see if Bob would finally appear.

As we exited the museum, there was Bob, happy as a lark. He had somehow missed me by the restrooms, couldn't find the group, toured the museum by himself, and joined those waiting outside.

He was "all smiles." Pat and I were "all frowns," but breathing sighs of relief. He had a great tour of the museum. Pat and I saw nothing!

Thanks a lot, Bob!

"TIE ONE ON!"

Before our trip to Greece, Bob had purchased a new pair of walking shoes. On his way to the elevator by himself at our nice hotel in Athens, he accidentally stepped on his shoelace just as the elevator door opened.

At the very next floor, more people got on the already-crowded elevator, pointed at Bob's untied shoelace, and said something in Greek. Bob smiled and nodded.

Again the door opened on the next floor, and another person entered, noticed Bob's shoelace, called his attention to it, and said something in a different language. Bob again smiled, as if to say he realized it was untied. However, because the elevator was crowded, it was impossible for him to do anything to remedy the situation.

The scene repeated itself at the next stop as more people entered. The other passengers smiled knowingly as if to say, "We've already tried to tell him."

Bob was embarrassed, but told me later that, in the small elevator, he felt like he was packed in a can of sardines. He believed that if he had tried to bend down and tie his shoe, they would need the "jaws of life" to extricate him from the bowels of the elevator.

As soon as Bob exited the elevator, he was able to tie his shoe.

Greece attracts tourists from all over the world, so several different language groups were represented in the large hotel. I was thinking how good it was that God didn't call us to be missionaries.

I'll stick to the English language, thank you. I do speak a "wee" bit of French ("oui, oui") and a little Spanish. Do you want to hear me count to 10 in Spanish?

KEEP YOUR EYES ON THAT LADY!

Do you think I look like a terrorist? Do I act like a terrorist? Do I think like a terrorist?

The Jeopardy answers to those three questions would be "No," "No," and "No."

Believe it or not, security employees in Istanbul, Turkey, targeted me as a potential threat.

Flying both directions on Turkish Airlines, we changed planes in Istanbul with only a few minutes to spare to continue our return flight to Chicago.

For some reason, security decided to open and search all of my carry-on luggage, including my small purse. There was a holdup because of one item in my purse. I was carrying an *EpiPen* which was acquired with a prescription. Bob is allergic to bee venom, and the pen contained epinephrine which is injected into one's thigh via a needle. The *EpiPen* I was carrying was actually a dual pack which was held together with a small metal clip.

The security personnel did not know what it was! One by one, the four or five authorities examined it.

Then they examined my camera, asking me to "empty" it. I simply removed the battery and returned it to the camera.

By this time, I was wondering if we were going to miss the plane. However, after much discussion, we were finally permitted to board the plane as the last passengers.

Of course, the whole episode was humorous—after we boarded the plane.

I confess that at least this time, Bob was with me and had not gone missing. I would have hated to see his picture on the side of a milk carton in Turkey!

WE'RE NOT ALONE WHEN IT COMES TO HUMOR

After Moses, the great leader of Israel, died, God put His right-hand man, Joshua, in charge. Before Joshua led the multitude of Israelites across the Jordan River to begin conquering the residents of the land God had promised them, the people said to Joshua: *"Whatever you have commanded us we will do, and wherever you send us we will go. Just as we fully obeyed Moses, so we will obey you"* (Joshua 1:16-17a).

I can picture Joshua holding back a snicker at the words, *"just as we fully obeyed Moses."*

The truth was that they were constantly disobeying Moses! Their disobedience led to grim consequences for the whole group numerous times. In fact, their stubborn disobedience resulted in their having to wander in the wilderness for 40 years as part of God's discipline.

Joshua might have wanted to excuse himself, and secretly have a good laugh at their response.

Yes, people are funny.

I wonder if God thinks I am "funny?" Do my expressions of love and commitment to Him hold up under the scrutiny of His Holy Spirit? Or is my level of obedience to Him shallow, partial, or . . . laughable?

When I tell God that I love Him and want to live according to His will, does He believe me, or does He excuse Himself, and secretly have a good laugh?

Does God think you are funny?

Think about it!

BOB'S FINAL THOUGHTS

I demand equal time regarding Judy's story about that museum in Athens.

First of all, I was never lost. I knew exactly where I was the whole time. I had seen Judy standing in the long line at the women's restroom. After promising her that I would wait close by, I looked down the hallway and saw a chair which had "welcome" written all over it. As I sat there, I never noticed Judy when she came out of the restroom.

Second, I even saw our tour guide and spoke to her, not realizing that I was thought to be "missing in action." The tour guide smiled at me but did not respond. I admitted to Judy, "I'm sure she probably mistook me for just another handsome stranger."

The bottom line to all of this, however, can be summed up in one of the greatest hymns ever written, "I once was lost, but now am found."

CHAPTER SIX

EYES WIDE OPEN
Bob Neuman

The two beautiful African-American children looked up at Judy and me as we approached the casket. "Did you know her?" one of them asked.

We replied that we did know Carolyn, the woman in the casket.

Pat, a friend of ours, and a co-worker of Carolyn's, introduced the two girls to us as Carolyn's granddaughters. We told them that we had known their grandmother for several years, and that she was a wonderful woman.

Then one of the girls earnestly asked, "Is she dead?"

Judy replied sympathetically, "Yes. She died."

"How did she die?" they asked in unison.

"She was very sick," Judy explained. Carolyn had been diagnosed with breast cancer about a year earlier, but succumbed after a valiant battle against the disease.

Trying to soften the blow, and obviously having been asked the same questions before we arrived at the funeral home, Pat spoke up and said to the girls, "She just closed her eyes and went to sleep."

Then, as Pat graciously introduced us to other family members, Judy overhead the girls talking with each other.

One of the girls remarked, "Well, then *I* just won't close *my* eyes!"

The other young lady emphatically added, "If *I* close *my* eyes, *I'll* just open them right up again!"

DON'T YOU WISH IT WERE THAT SIMPLE?

Trying to avoid death by refusing to close one's eyes is impossible. Both the Old and New Testaments of the Bible tell us that death is inevitable.

One does not have to read very far in Genesis, the first book of the Bible, before a phrase—*"and he died"*—appears over and over again. Genesis 5:5, 8, and 11 state, *"So all the days that Adam lived were nine hundred and thirty years, and he died. . . . So all the days of Seth were nine hundred and twelve years, and he died. . . . So all the days of Enosh were nine hundred and five years, and he died."* Are you beginning to see the picture?

An Old Testament writer phrased it this way in Ecclesiastes 3:1-2, *"There is an appointed time for everything. And there is a time for every event under heaven—a time to give birth and a time to die; a time to plant and a time to uproot what is planted."*

The writer to the Hebrews wrote these words, *"And inasmuch as it is appointed for men to die once and after this comes judgment"* (Hebrews 9:27).

The great Old Testament prophet Isaiah made this declaration at the command of God: *"The grass withers, the flower fades, when the breath of the Lord blows upon it; surely the people are grass"* (Isaiah 40:7).

ONE DOES NOT HAVE TO BE A BOTANIST

I remember the excitement our older daughter experienced when she was in elementary school. The class was learning the truth about planting seeds.

Her teacher had lined the window sill with a number of little Styrofoam cups in which various seeds had been planted.

He explained to the class that, in order for the seed to bring forth life, it really had to die first.

SO, WE'VE "GONE TO SEED," HUH?

What a simple, yet profound, analogy.

Even Jesus chose a seed to illustrate the truth about dying. He proclaimed, *". . . unless a grain of wheat falls into the earth and dies, it remains alone; but if it dies, it bears much fruit"* (John 12:24). Is it just me, or does everybody who plants a few zucchini seeds end up with bushels of them to give away?

A CHURCH ORDINANCE
PRESENTS A SIMILAR PICTURE

Whenever most evangelical churches conduct baptismal services, the pastor will speak of the waters of baptism, declaring that when the baptismal candidate is placed under the water, it is symbolic of being buried with Christ. Then, as the individual is brought up from the waters, that speaks of being raised with Christ, to walk in newness of life. The Apostle Paul penned these words about Jesus: *"having been buried with him in baptism, in which you were also raised with him through your faith in the working of God who raised him from the dead"* (Colossians 2:12).

Job, the godly suffering man of the Old Testament, pondered the topic of death and eternal life. Here is the testimony as found in Job 19:25-27: *"As for me, I know that my Redeemer lives, and at the last He will take His stand on the earth. Even after my skin is destroyed, yet from my flesh I shall see God; whom I myself shall behold, and whom my eyes will see and not another; my heart faints within me!"*

HERE'S THE GOOD NEWS!

Jesus arrived in town after the death of a dear friend named Lazarus. He said to Martha, Lazarus' sister, *". . . Your brother will rise again"* (John 11:23).

Martha responded that she believed he would rise again in the resurrection at the last day, but Jesus countered, *". . . I am the resurrection and the life; he who believes in Me will live even if he dies"* (John 11:25). Then Jesus illustrated this mini-sermon by actually raising Lazarus from the dead.

The good news about our friend, Carolyn, is that she had put her trust in Jesus Christ as her personal Savior. That means that she, too, will live again.

When we see Carolyn in heaven someday, her eyes will be wide open, reflecting the brightness of our glorious Savior, Jesus Christ.

And, thank God, there will be no more closed eyes!

BOB'S FINAL THOUGHTS

Rev. Dwight L. Moody, the late famous Chicago evangelist, was born on February 5, 1837, and passed away on December 22, 1899.

In one of his sermons he announced, "Someday you will read that D. L. Moody is dead. Don't you believe a word of it. At that moment I shall be more alive than I am now. I shall have gone up higher, that's all—out of this old clay tenement into a house that is immortal; a body that death cannot touch, that sin cannot taint, a body fashioned like unto His glorious body. . . . I was born of the flesh in 1837. I was born of the Spirit in 1856. That which is born of the flesh may die. That which is born of the Spirit will live forever."

It does not sound like Rev. Moody was afraid of closing his eyes, does it?

But how can you be sure that you will live again? It is really as simple as A, B, C.

Admit that you are a sinner. *"There is none righteous, not even one. . . for all have sinned and fall short of the glory of God"* (Romans 3:10, 23. See also Romans 5:8 and 6:23).

Believe in Jesus. This means to put your trust in Him as your only hope of salvation. *"For God so loved the world, that He gave*

His only begotten Son, that whoever believes in Him shall not perish, but have eternal life" (John 3:16. See also John 14:6).

Confess that Jesus is your Lord. *". . . if you confess with your mouth Jesus as Lord, and believe in your heart that God raised Him from the dead, you will be saved"* (Romans 10:9. See verse 10 as well).

CHAPTER SEVEN

"WILL THAT BE ONE DIP OR TWO?"

Judy Neuman

The advertised special at the restaurant was: ANY THREE APPETIZERS FOR 10.99—WITH <u>TWO</u> <u>DIPS</u>. When I saw the words, "TWO DIPS," I knew that special had our names written all over it!

It was late at night, so Bob and I decided to split the appetizer and call it "dinner." We were so hungry, and the food was so delicious, that we polished it off in record time—every crumb!

When our young server returned to our table and saw our empty plates, she smiled broadly, and enthusiastically exclaimed, "Good job!"

After she left, Bob and I looked at each other and burst into laughter. She had spoken those words as if we were both toddlers who had eaten all of the vegetables on our plates!

AHA! The tone of her response was another sign that we are morphing into . . . (Hold on to your seats, and hear the scary music playing in the background) . . . OLD FOLKS!

In my mind, I am still that young, thin girl skipping along life's pathway, oblivious to the detours, and pot holes in the road that lies ahead.

But when I look into the mirror, I see the changes that the passing of time has brought. Yes, I have hit a few of those potholes, and have taken some detours, including picking up a "second dip" many years ago when I married Bob. (Bob made me write that line. He says his favorite type of humor is the self-deprecating kind!)

SIGNS ALONG THE WAY

The signposts along our pathways are ever changing. I remember when the signpost read: "<u>This Way to First Grade</u>." Orientation was held in the school gymnasium. My friend from church, David, was sitting next to me, and we were afraid of the unknown! But we ended up in the same classroom, and had a wonderful teacher, Mrs. Holt. First grade turned out to be great.

However, at my first parent-teacher conference, Mrs. Holt told my mom that I was "in the doghouse." When my mom repeated to me what the teacher said, I asked, "What is 'the doghouse'?" Now, whenever I don't understand a word or phrase, I ask Bob. But when he introduced me to "Google," Google replaced him!

The reason I was "in the doghouse" was because my best girl friend and I spent a <u>long time</u> in the restroom making bubbles in the sink with the powdered soap from the dispenser. (I was in the doghouse in college for the same reason . . . just kidding!)

RULES OF THE ROAD

Quite a memorable signpost along the way said, "<u>This Way to Driving School</u>."

There was no Driver's Education class at my high school until after I learned to drive. (Bob said that's probably why they decided such a class was necessary!). Therefore, my dad became my instructor. Every lesson left him hyperventilating, and may also have been the cause of his rapidly-graying hair.

One day, he asked me to back up the car close to the barn so that he could load some bales of hay into the trunk. Dad's first mistake was asking me to do this. His second mistake was to stand between the car and the barn as I backed up. The car had a stick-shift (which I had not yet mastered), and I let the clutch out too quickly causing the car to lurch backwards. To keep himself from having his legs cut off at the knees, Dad quickly jumped onto the trunk before I hit the barn! Although I love to travel, I admit that was the shortest and "scariest" trip I ever have taken. Now you understand why Bob is reluctant to let me drive on long trips, even though our car has an automatic transmission.

"OVER THE HILL?"

An extremely shocking signpost in my life read, "<u>This Is Your 30th Birthday</u>." By this time I was a pastor's wife, a mother of two beautiful little girls, and living a wonderful, fulfilled life. But this birthday was more of a wake-up call than any birthday I've had since then. People were beginning to call me, "Mrs. Neuman!" GOOD GRIEF! I was no longer perceived to be the happy, go-lucky college girl of my past. Now I was expected to be . . . AN ADULT!

Well, now that signpost is far behind me, and all of the signposts far ahead of me have to do with what is commonly called, "Old Age."

Strangely enough, I love this stretch of road on life's highway, even though I have more physical concerns than I did "way back then." Bob says, "I love this period of life as well, especially the senior citizen discounts, and Social Security!"

UNCHANGING SIGNPOSTS

As I've passed the various signposts in life, one truth has remained constant, and that is the fact that God was—and is—present! He has made every transition in my life "do-able." I made it through first grade *by His grace*. I learned to drive (and Dad survived) *by His grace*. I made it through my thirties and beyond, *by His grace*. And now I am facing "old age," *by His grace*!

The Bible, God's *inspired* Word, urges us all to allow God to be of utmost importance in our thoughts, our lives, and our hearts at every juncture in life. Ecclesiastes 12:1 states, *"Remember also your Creator in the days of your youth, before the evil days come and the years draw near when you will say, 'I have no delight in them'."*

Whether you realize it or not, God has been involved in your life since before you were born! That's a deep, comforting thought. The God of this universe cared about you, and each person that He ever created, from the very beginning.

In a prayer to God, King David said, *"For You formed my inward parts; You wove me in my mother's womb. I will give thanks to You, for I am fearfully and wonderfully made; Wonderful are Your works, and my soul knows it very well. My frame was not hidden from You, when I was made in secret, and skillfully wrought in the depths of the earth; Your eyes have seen my unformed substance; and in Your book were all written the days that were ordained for me, when as yet there was not one of them"* (Psalm 139:13-16).

So God was present in your life even before your body began to form in your mother's womb. Awesome! God has been committed to you and to me before we even knew about Him.

THE BEND IN THE ROAD
IS NOT THE END OF THE ROAD

As King David matured in life, he saw God as his shepherd, who guided him through every circumstance, who loved him in every situation, and who would give him eternal life. The 23rd Psalm declares, *"Surely goodness and lovingkindness will follow me all the days of my life, and I will dwell in the house of the Lord forever"* (Psalm 23:6).

David also wrote, *"O God, You have taught me from my youth, and I still declare Your wondrous deeds. And even when I am old and gray, O God, do not forsake me, until I declare Your strength to this generation, Your power to all who are to come"* (Psalm 71:17-18).

David knew that God was committed to him throughout his whole life, and David was willing to commit himself back to God. He was so excited by God's presence that he wanted to live long enough to tell the younger generation about the power and greatness of God!

What signpost in life is staring you in the face right now? Whether you are young or old, God is committed to you, so much so that *"God so loved the world, that He gave His only begotten Son, that whoever believes in Him, shall not perish, but have eternal life"* (John 3:16).

Please don't travel any farther in life until you read the signpost directly ahead of you on which God's Son, Jesus Christ, says to you, *"I am the way, and the truth, and the life; no one comes to the Father but through Me"* (John 14:6).

Jesus is not only *with you* on the path of life, He *is* the path, the *only way* to the Father.

BOB'S FINAL THOUGHTS

Amen!

Sorry!

My mind was busy thinking of those late-night appetizers!

CHAPTER EIGHT

BLUEBERRY BUCKETS AND A DIME JAR

Bob Neuman

When our daughters were little, we fled the city for a day of blueberry picking at a farm near DeMotte, Indiana. That was our first foray into the world of blueberry picking.

When we arrived at the farm, the lady asked us, "How many buckets will you need?"

I thought, "Well, duh! There are four of us!" Instead, I politely replied, "Four."

Carrying our large buckets, we headed off in search of our prey.

The four of us picked, and picked, and picked. We picked, and we picked, and we picked. We picked, and we picked, and we picked.

Oh, wait a minute. Did I just mention that we picked?

After what seemed like hours of picking, we noticed that the bottom of each bucket was barely covered. It was at that point, as I gazed at our meager "offering," that I wished we were filling our buckets with apples, cantaloupes, or large watermelons instead of blueberries.

We finally consolidated all four buckets into one, had it weighed, and paid the amount based upon that weight.

For a long season thereafter, we enjoyed the "fruit" of our labor, as Judy made blueberry pancakes and various desserts.

An ad for Greyhound Lines, the bus company, suggests, "Take the bus and leave the driving to us."

We agreed that, next time, we would "buy the blueberries and leave the picking to somebody else." We departed that day from "Blueberry Hill" without experiencing very many "thrills." We couldn't even fill one bucket!

IT BEGAN IN CHILDHOOD

Let me begin this part of the story by telling you that my childhood "devotional reading" consisted largely of comic books, and what we called the "funny papers" in our local newspaper.

Growing up poor, I was especially drawn to comics like "Richie Rich," a wealthy boy who was born with a silver spoon in his mouth the size of the bucket on a backhoe. OH, NO! I can't get away from buckets, can I?

In addition to Richie Rich, I was mesmerized by a web-footed, aquatic bird named Scrooge McDuck.

My memories of Scrooge are two-fold. First, I remember him frolicking in his vault of money (cash and coins), with the depth of his amassed holdings measured by foot markers on the wall in his large safe.

The second memory was that he always was on guard to protect his money from a trio of thieves, known as, "The Beagle Boys."

Maybe it was these images that led to my life-long attempt to save money. I'm sure we can identify with the words of the Old Testament wisdom writer who observed, *"Cast but a glance at riches, and they are gone, for they will surely sprout wings, and fly off to the sky like an eagle"* (Proverbs 23:5).

That biblical wisdom is illustrated by a little poem I learned years ago:

"That money talks,

I'll not deny.

I heard it once:

It said 'Goodbye'!"

"BEN" THERE . . . DONE THAT!

On the other hand, that same biblical author penned, *"Dishonest money dwindles away, but he who gathers money little by little makes it grow"* (Proverbs 13:11).

Those words sound so much like Benjamin (Ben) Franklin who opined that "A penny saved is a penny earned."

Such advice about gathering money "little by little," and "a penny saved is a penny earned," led me to a life-time investment in what I call, "hog futures."

But "hog futures" for me has nothing to do with the selling of "pork bellies" on the Chicago Mercantile Exchange.

"Hog futures" refers to my collection of several piggy banks and other containers for my savings. I became a diversified investor, learning not to put all of my pods into one pig, so to speak.

At various times my "bank" was a can, a jar, or a large plastic Coca-Cola bottle.

Because I use the term, "hog futures," my rule of thumb is that the piggy bank is untouchable. In fact, it is as "unclean" to me as a real pig or hog would be to devout followers of either the Jewish or Muslim faiths!

Once the piggy bank is full, I "butcher" it. Now, before you report me to the ASPCA (the American Society for the Prevention of Cruelty to Animals), let me add that the butchering consists of removing the "plug" from the bottom of the bank.

If said "pig" does not have a plug to release its contents, then I practice "safe surgery" by inserting a knife in the money slot as I gradually disembowel the entire pig. Just like the disclaimer in the movies, I assure you that "No animals are harmed in this process."

Our two daughters have tried to follow this example, although our youngest, Lori, has a harder time waiting for the pig to be fattened. But, once a family member fills a bank, we each try to guess how much money is in the container.

LET'S GET BACK TO THE DIME JAR

A number of years ago, our youngest daughter, Lori, and her former husband, vacationed in Colorado. When they returned, they brought Judy and me a souvenir. It was a small jar that had a colorful Colorado scene pictured on it, along with the words, "Colorado Mountain Seeds."

The jar contained chocolate-covered shelled sunflower seeds. Man, I'm sure glad we didn't have to fill our buckets with sunflower seeds!

The jar stood about 3½ inches high, and was about 8¼ inches in circumference. After eating the contents of the jar, which, sad to say, went to "waist" (unfortunately ours), I salvaged the jar and it became my next "hog futures" project.

I decided to fill it with dimes, not realizing how long it takes to fill even a small jar with thin dimes, much like filling our large buckets with small blueberries. But, once that job was accomplished, I butchered it, and decided to fill it next time with quarters.

I do have a confession to make. I'm sorry that, when it comes to filling piggy banks, silver dollars are no longer in general circulation.

An old saying declares that, "Patience is a virtue." If that is true, then savers like me have to be among the most virtuous people on Planet Earth!

IT'S ALL ABOUT PERSPECTIVE

I believe that a major lesson I have learned over the years about money is to keep everything in perspective. Jesus warned, *"Do not store up for yourselves treasures on earth, where moth and vermin destroy, and where thieves break in and steal. But store up for yourselves treasures in heaven, where moth and vermin do not destroy and where thieves do not break in and steal. For where your treasure is, there your heart will be also"* (Matthew 6:19-21).

Jesus taught us, *"But seek first his kingdom and his righteousness, and all these things will be given to you as well"* (Matthew 6:33).

The Old Testament emphasized, *"But remember the Lord your God, for it is he who gives you the ability to produce wealth"* (Deuteronomy 8:18).

Another lesson I learned is a truth found in Acts 20:35. The Apostle Paul wrote, *"In everything I did, I showed you that by this kind of hard work we must help the weak, remembering the words the Lord Jesus himself said, 'It is more blessed to give than to receive'."*

Dr. Charles W. Koller, a professor of mine while I was a student at Trinity Evangelical Divinity School in Deerfield, Illinois, referred to this as "The supreme beatitude." It is the only beatitude attributed to Jesus that has the adjective "more" attached to it.

The greatest lesson that I learned about money is that it all comes from God, and I am responsible to return a portion of it to Him. The Bible admonishes us to *"Honor the Lord with your wealth, with the firstfruits of all your crops; then your barns will be filled to overflowing, and your vats will brim with new wine"* (Proverbs 3:9-10).

Saving money is great, but we must hold on to it lightly. The Bible itself warns, *"If anyone does not provide for his relatives, and especially for his immediate family, he has denied the faith, and is worse than an unbeliever"* (1 Timothy 5:8).

It also reminds us that, *"A good man leaves an inheritance for his children's children . . ."* (Proverbs 13:22a).

You also will discover that the Bible contains instructions about caring for the poor and needy among us.

Keep investing in hog futures, but keep all things—even money—in perspective!

BOB'S FINAL THOUGHTS

Currently, I have three banks that are being "fattened up." In 2019 I accepted "The $5 Challenge." Each time I get a five dollar bill in change, I put it in a bank. My current receptacle is a large aluminum Coca-Cola bank that my youngest daughter, Lori, purchased for me. At the end of each month, I cash the contents at my local bank. Then I immediately write a check for that amount, and send it to my credit union savings account.

The second bank is a large jar. It was given to me by the late Mary Jane Lionberg, a member of the church I pastored. It "talks," so each time that money is inserted, it states the amount, and gives me the total in the bank. That bank is used only for quarters, so I might hear something like this: "Twenty-five cents. Thirty dollars and seventy-five cents." It, too, is in the process of being fattened.

My final bank is a clear acrylic piggy bank. It is reserved only for nickels and dimes.

Okay, but what about the "penny saved is a penny earned" thing?

I keep pennies in my pocket for purchases that require one to four cents, such a $1.11 or $7.93. That means that the change I get back will involve nickels, dimes or quarters or a combination thereof.

Yes, there is a method to my madness but, after all, saving money is all about being methodical and disciplined.

Try it. You will like it!

CHAPTER NINE

"WHAT DID YOU JUST SAY, SALLY?"

Judy Neuman

Our friend, Sally, had her hair in a ponytail. I commented on how long her hair had grown. It was at that moment that our unplanned comedy sketch began:

SALLY: "If I had worn my hair down today, I would have looked like 'Saskatchewan'!"

JUDY: "You mean 'Sasquatch'?" (also known as "Big Foot!"). "A 'Saskatchewan' is a Canadian, which might be just as scary." (Just kidding, Canadian friends!)

SALLY: "Isn't 'Saskatchewan' a Chinese dish?" (She was thinking of the word "Szechwan.")

We both had a good laugh about our humorous distortion of the English language. I was reminded of a quotation by Mark Twain, the great American humorist, who said, "The difference between the right word and the almost right word is the difference between 'lightning' and 'lightning bug'."

I REMEMBER WHEN . . . .

One of my childhood memories includes a visit to a funhouse where numerous mirrors reflected my image in various ways. In one mirror, I looked three feet tall and three feet wide with a flat head and stretched-out face. That would have been a strange profile picture for a Facebook page if Mark Zuckerberg had invented it back then.

Another mirror portrayed me as being ultra tall and pencil thin. I think that someone should manufacture this mirror for home use . . . or one that always answers, "YOU ARE," when asked, "Who's the fairest in the land?"

In this scenario, the visual distortion was all about fun.

Some distortions can be deadly! Picture the poor duck who is lured to its death by following the sound of a hunter's "duck call" (Just ask Uncle Si and the gang at "Duck Dynasty" about this). The duck may be fooled into thinking he is hearing that "cute chick"— er, duckling—he met the day before.

He is wrong! And that duck will never be right . . . or wrong . . . again. He simply will be a delicious entrée served with orange sauce at someone's dinner table.

OUT OF "WHACK!"

In certain circumstances, our perception can easily become distorted. After a serious car accident in the 1960's, I found myself sitting in the roof of our upside-down older Oldsmobile. (I loved that car!). For a few seconds, I couldn't get my bearings, and wasn't even aware that my small spot in that part of my world was upside down! Thank God that nobody, including me, was badly hurt in that accident!

Various types of distortions are common in our everyday lives. One dictionary definition of "distortion" is ". . . a change, twist, or exaggeration that makes something appear different from the way it really is. You can distort an image, a thought, or even an idea."

Some modern examples are an airbrushed photo of a beautiful model in a magazine, the "brainwashing" of prisoners of war, or the mirage of an oasis in a scorching desert.

SPIRITUALLY SPEAKING

Spiritual truths can be distorted.

Jesus Christ encountered spiritual distortion in His own day when some people believed that He was from Satan instead of having been sent by God.

One common distorted belief nowadays is that God exists solely for our comfort, happiness, and prosperity. What a different picture the Bible presents!

Do you remember Shadrach, Meshach and Abednego whose experiences are recorded in the biblical book of Daniel? When they refused to bow down and worship a golden image of King Nebuchadnezzar, they were threatened by death in a fiery trap, called a furnace.

Their reply to the king was interesting. They said, *"If we are thrown into the blazing furnace, the God we serve is able to save us from it, and He will rescue us from your hand, O King. But even if He does not, we want you to know, O King, that we will not serve your gods or worship the image of gold you have set up"* (Daniel 3:17-18). Words underlined were by the writer for emphasis.

We heard a great sermon years ago by a missionary who emphasized these points.

. They believed that God was able to save them.

. They had faith that God would save them.

. They were committed to God even if He did not save them!

The reason for their "civil disobedience" was that God explicitly commanded them not to bow down to any image or idol, but to worship only the living God.

In the end, God miraculously protected them in the fiery furnace, and they didn't even smell like smoke when they came out alive, even though that furnace had been heated seven times hotter than usual! They were willing to obey God no matter what!

ANOTHER GREAT EXAMPLE

The Apostle Paul experienced many miraculous deliverances. However, he was also beaten, stoned, shipwrecked, and imprisoned, simply because he was preaching the truth about Jesus. Throughout all of his sorrows and discomfort, he stayed firm in his faith, even when God did not intervene.

A person with a distorted perspective believes, "Life is all about me, my circumstances, my happiness, and my comfort!"

Faithful, committed Christians of the Bible did not think that way. What God said, they believed. What God wanted done, they did! And they were willing to live their lives according to God's instructions, even if doing that brought them pain, ridicule, discomfort, poverty, or imprisonment for their faith. They were willing to postpone receiving their rewards until their face-to-face reunion with Jesus in heaven. The joy and peace they experienced on earth were by-products of a close relationship with God, and obedience to His Word.

BEWARE OF DISTORTIONS!

Distortions are pervasive! God's Word to the prophet Isaiah included this warning, *"Woe to those who call evil good and good evil, who put darkness for light and light for darkness, who put bitter for sweet and sweet for bitter"* (Isaiah 5:20).

If the whole world says that a certain lifestyle, behavior, or way of thinking is right, but God says it is wrong, to whom will we listen? A committed Christian will listen to God.

The Apostle Paul admonished us in Romans 3:4, *". . . Let God be true, and every man a liar. . . ."*

A distorted view of God's truth can be eternally deadly!

Here's an undistorted truth to which we can freely respond: *"For God so loved the world that He gave His one and only Son, that whoever believes in Him shall not perish but have eternal life"* (John 3:16). You will notice that we use this verse often in our writings. That's because it is such an important truth!

BOB'S FINAL WORD

My first profile picture on Facebook was that of "Quark," the conniving Ferengi from the Star Trek television series. Strangely enough, nobody ever questioned me as to whether that was what I really looked like. I'm glad that they didn't. To be honest with you, I think Quark is quite a handsome alien!

CHAPTER TEN

AUTHOR, AUTHOR!

Bob Neuman

Several years ago, our family celebrated the birthday of our former son-in-law at a nice restaurant that featured Chinese, Japanese, and Thai cuisine. The six of us deliberately ordered different entrees so that we each could have a good sampling of the food, as well as leftovers to take home. "Leftovers" is a popular word in our family.

After the meal, we opened our fortune cookies, and read the short messages. We do not direct our lives by such fortunes, but we were amused to see that the note in my cookie read, "You will become an accomplished writer."

What if I worked at the factory that made those cookies, and had inserted a message that read, "Ewe well bekum and akomplished righter." Do you think I would qualify for that title?

WRITE ON!

We reflected upon that statement then, and even later. For several years, Judy and I had written *"An encouraging word,"* a monthly inspirational newsletter. Had I become an accomplished writer? Had Judy? That is for our readers to decide.

Judi, a friend of ours, not to be confused with my wife, Judy, sent us an e-mail in which she wrote, "Thanks for the copy of *'An encouraging word.'* As usual I enjoyed it very much. I certainly hope you're keeping all of these to write in a book someday. I'll buy a copy for sure."

Well, I now know that we would sell at least one book, but I don't think that such a sale would qualify me as an accomplished writer . . . nor get me on the *New York Times* Best Seller list.

Judy, on the other hand, has written several books. You see, since high school, she has kept a daily diary. Sad to say, Judy adamantly declares that they are NOT for sale!

QUIZ TIME: WHO SAID IT?

Match each famous person with the quotation attributed to him:

1) Albert Einstein (1879—1955; German-born Swiss-American physicist)

2) Will Rogers (1879—1935; Cherokee cowboy, humorist, social commentator)

3) George Burns (1896—1996; American actor, comedian; straight man to wife Gracie Allen)

4) Abraham Lincoln (1809—1865; 16th President of the United States)

5) Winston Churchill (1874—1965; British politician; two-time Prime Minister of England)

(6) Mark Twain (1835—1910; Real name: Samuel Clemens; American author and humorist)

(a) "Common-looking people are the best in the world: that's the reason the Lord made so many of them."

(b) "I am fond of pigs. Dogs look up to us. Cats look down on us. Pigs treat us as equals."

(c) "Put your hand on a hot stove for a minute, and it seems like an hour. Sit with a pretty girl for an hour, and it seems like a minute. That's relativity."

(d) "A classic is something that everyone wants to have read and nobody wants to read."

(e) "The secret of a good sermon is to have a good beginning and a good ending; and to have the two as close together as possible."

(f) "Live in such a way that you would not be ashamed to sell your parrot to the town gossip."

READ ON!

Our friend, Rich, loves to read biographies and autobiographies.

Judy reads murder mysteries. If I die, and the circumstances surrounding my death are questionable, please remember this bit of information.

From childhood, our daughter, Natalie, has been a voracious reader. Several years ago we purchased a figurine based on the artistic drawings of Sister Maria Innocentia Hummel, the talented Bavarian Catholic nun. It shows a little girl sitting on the floor, totally absorbed in reading a book. It is called, "Bookworm," and it captures Natalie's personality so well that it will be part of our family's legacy to her. She jokes that, after we die, she will sell it at a garage sale for a nickel. After a remark like that, we may decide to give the whole inheritance to Lori. (It's possible that Judy's diaries might also be a part of Natalie's garage sale!)

MAY I RECOMMEND A BOOK TO YOU?

To be honest, the book that I would recommend to you is *my favorite book,* and it is unique in so many ways. Here are some facts about that book:

It was written by 40 different authors during a period of over 1500 years.

The authors included kings, peasants, philosophers, poets, fishermen, statesmen, and scholars.

They wrote while living in wildernesses, dungeons, palaces, or in exile, as well as during times of war and peace.

It is a book written on three continents (Asia, Africa, and Europe), and in three languages (Hebrew, Aramaic, and Greek).

The United Bible Societies report that this book, in whole or in part, has been translated into more than 3,324 languages, including complete Old or New Testaments in 2,189 languages.

And it is the BEST-SELLING BOOK EVER!

In case you have not figured it out yet, it is THE BIBLE, God's Word, and as an old chorus declares, "Yes, that's the Book for me!"

David, considered to be Israel's greatest king, wrote about this book, declaring, *"Your word is a lamp to my feet and a light to my path"* (Psalm 119:105).

Jesus Christ, the central figure of the Bible, challenged people in His day with these words, *"You search the Scriptures because you think that in them you have eternal life; it is these that testify about Me"* (John 5:39).

Why not pick up a copy of the Bible, and enjoy the greatest book ever written? Some people call it, "The Good Book." It is not only "good," but it also is God's love letter to us!

It is such a wonderful book, that I once shared with a group seven ways that we should use our Bibles.

1. Read it.
2. Study it.
3. Obey it.
4. Memorize it.
5. Pray it.
6. Sing it.
7. Share it.

BOB'S FINAL THOUGHTS

After we finished the birthday meal, and had all of our leftovers properly divided, the waitress held the bill over the center of the table. She reminded me of a National Basketball Association referee getting ready for the tip-off at a basketball game.

My family members glanced at each other and, as I reached for my wallet, our son-in-law, Tim, extended his hand, took the bill . . . and handed it to me as he quipped, "Give it to the writer!"

I console myself that, at least on that day, my writing was worth something to the restaurant!

NOW BACK TO THE QUIZ. The answers to the quiz are as follows:

    1—C

    2—F

    3—E

    4—A

    5—B

    6—D

The quotation by George Burns about a good sermon was sent to us by our friend, Marcie. Knowing that I am a minister, she wrote these words underneath the quotation: "Just trying to be helpful!"

CHAPTER ELEVEN

EASTER: WHAT IS IT?

Judy Neuman

Every year, as Easter approaches, the stores are well stocked with cuddly Easter bunnies, chocolate-covered marshmallow eggs (Bob's favorite!), and colorful baskets filled with noticeably fake grass!

But for the Christian, the Easter season represents far more! Good Friday commemorates the death of Jesus Christ, the Son of God, and Easter Sunday, known as "Resurrection Sunday," is the celebration of His empty grave.

Jesus' death and resurrection proves that He is God, the *living* God, not a dead, powerless one.

"IT IS WRITTEN!"

Chapter 53 of the book of Isaiah in the Bible takes a fascinating look at the death of Jesus. This chapter is especially interesting because it was written between 600 and 700 years before Jesus was even born! God Himself gave the prophet Isaiah a glimpse into the future.

Verse 10 of that chapter contains a puzzling statement about God, the Lord, and His only begotten Son, Jesus Christ: *"But the Lord was pleased to crush Him, putting Him to grief. . . ."*

A few years ago I wrote a poem as I pondered the meaning of that verse.

"THE LORD WAS PLEASED!"

Lord, how could it have pleased You

to see Your dear Son crushed,

and broken by the unleashed crowd,

their angry faces flushed?

And how could there be pleasure

in the anguish of His soul,

with a crown of thorns thrust on His head,

the rough-hewn cross His goal?

Could joy be birthed from pain

when Jesus hung against the sky,

and He was put to grief

as He died with one last cry?

"It is finished!" rang the words

as they echoed from the past.

"He's dead!" they yelled. Some laughed and said,
"We're rid of Him at last!"

Where's the pleasure of my Savior's death?
For an answer I'm at a loss.
Is the clue contained in Jesus' words,
He uttered from the cross?

What was finished there, I queried,
as evil prevailed that day?
When I pondered this within my heart,
the Father seemed to say:

"My Son's short life was fervent
in His obedience to Me.
Yes, my child, I'm very pleased
with His faithful ministry!"

"It is true His heart was tempted
by Satan, the self-willed one,
but my Son's devotion triumphed,
and selflessly He won!"

"My only Son was willing
to go the second mile

and leave His home in heaven
to suffer on earth awhile."

As God spoke to me in whispers
of wisdom tried and true,
I began to see how joy could come
from what our Lord went through.

Though to some, the cross meant failure,
it was heaven's victory
over sin and death and sorrow
in the lives of you and me.

The power of Satan over us
was broken at the cross.
We can be forgiven now,
our gain is Satan's loss!

Oh, yes, I feel the joy of God
Who heard the angels sing
as Jesus rose up from the dead
to be our coming King!

Now I know why God was pleased,
although it brought Him pain.

Eternal life is mine today,

for Jesus lives again!

© Judith Crane Neuman

WHAT'S YOUR TAKE
ON ALL OF THIS, JESUS?
Bob Neuman

Hebrews 11 has been called, "The Hall of Fame in the Bible," since it contains the exploits of faith of the great men and women of Scripture. It not only presents those who experienced great victories and were delivered from the jaws of death, but gives testimony of those who also "died by faith."

I believe we get a glimpse of the way Jesus faced, and endured the cross in the first two verses of Hebrews 12:

"Therefore, since we have so great a cloud of witnesses surrounding us, let us also lay aside every encumbrance and the sin which so easily entangles us, and let us run with endurance the race that is set before us, fixing our eyes on Jesus, the author and perfecter of faith, who for the joy set before Him endured the cross, despising the shame, and has sat down at the right hand of the throne of God" (Hebrews 12:1-2).

BOB'S FINAL THOUGHTS

One Easter Sunday, Judy decided to wear a two-piece yellow suit to church. She loved that outfit. Thinking that she really looked great, she bounded down the stairs of our home where I was seated at the kitchen counter. Looking at me with a pleased smile on her face, she asked "How do I look, Bob?"

I glanced up and, without hesitation, replied, "Why, Judy, you look like a marshmallow Peep!" (People wonder how Judy has remained married to me for so long when they read true stories like this!)

CHAPTER TWELVE

A CASE OF "SAMMY-ITIS!"

Bob Neuman

Over the course of our marriage, Judy and I have owned several cats. Or, rather, let's be honest, they have owned us!

I can't say in biblical terms that our felines have been *"as numerous as the stars in the sky and the sand on the seashore"* (Genesis 22:17). Nor could their number be, in the words of Revelation 5:11, *"thousands upon thousands."*

It just seems that way. We have been blessed with an abundance of cats, and each of them has had its own personality.

Let me introduce you to "KoKo," who could be the spokesperson, oops "spokescat," for the stereotypical "scaredy cat." She was a beautiful, part Siamese cat who would jump at her own shadow. Because of her "shadow phobia," I guess it's good that they chose a groundhog to determine how long winter would last.

Koko's best cat friend was "Sammy," the star of this newsletter. She was a feminine, sleek, black cat.

On many occasions, we heard Sammy in the basement meowing up a storm. Upon discovering her problem, we came up with a name for it: "Sammy-itis."

That was our non-psychiatric term for her symptom of "cat anxiety." At that time, Sammy and KoKo shared a large dispenser, in which Judy faithfully placed dry cat food. Another apparatus dispensed fresh water.

However, if the food dispenser was less than a quarter full, Sammy-itis kicked in, and that feminine, sleek, black cat began her caterwauling.

In our defense, Judy and I never let a cat starve to death, or die from dehydration. But Sammy feared it might happen to her. When she saw her food level starting to get low, she thought she needed to warn us of her upcoming demise.

Is Sammy-itis a condition exclusive to Sammy?

I don't believe so. Many times, Judy and I are stricken with a human case of it when we worry about some potential problem.

Realizing that we are worrying unnecessarily, we make full eye contact with each other, and say in unison, "Meeeeeooooowwwww."

A DIVINE PRESCRIPTION

Here is how Eugene H. Peterson renders the words of the Apostle Paul in his paraphrase of the Bible, called *The Message:* *"Don't fret or worry. Instead of worrying, pray. Let petitions and praises shape your worries into prayers, letting God know your concerns. Before you know it, a sense of God's wholeness, everything coming together for good, will come and settle you down. It's wonderful what happens when Christ displaces worry at the center of your life"* (Philippians 4:7-8).

FROM THE FELINE TO THE BOVINE

I came across an anonymous poem many years ago. I believe it reveals that, not only cats and human beings, but also cows, suffer from their own form of Sammy-itis.

> "The worried cow would have lived 'til now,
>
> If she had saved her breath;
>
> But she feared the hay wouldn't last all day,
>
> And she mooed herself to death!"

FROM THE FELINE AND THE BOVINE
TO THE SUBLIME!

Let's return to the words from the Apostle Paul above. D. L. Moody, the late great Chicago evangelist, succinctly summarized it as follows:

> "Careful for nothing,
>
> prayerful for everything,
>
> thankful for anything."

Jesus Himself recognized our tendency to worry by declaring in Matthew 6:25-34, *"Therefore I tell you, do not worry about your life, what you will eat or drink; or about your body, what you will wear. Is not life more important than food, and the body more important than clothes? Look at the birds of the air; they do not sow or reap or store away in barns, and yet your heavenly Father feeds them. Are you not much more valuable than they? Who of you by worrying can add a single hour to his life? And why do you worry about clothes? See how the lilies of the field grow. They do not labor or spin. Yet I tell you that not even Solomon in all his splendor was dressed like one of these. If that is how God clothes the grass of the field, which is here today and tomorrow is thrown into the fire, will he not much more clothe you, O you of little faith? So do not worry, saying, 'What shall we eat?' or 'What shall we drink?' or 'What shall we wear?' For the pagans run after all these things, and your heavenly Father knows that you need them. But seek first his kingdom and his righteousness, and all these things will be given to you as well. Therefore do not worry about tomorrow, for tomorrow will worry about itself. Each day has enough trouble of its own."*

So Sammy . . . and Bob and Judy . . . and YOU, too . . . quit your meowing.

We have a loving Father who cares for us, and who promises to provide for us as we seek Him first.

BOB'S FINAL THOUGHTS

Let me conclude with two stories. The first one was told by an early American preacher, the late Rev. Henry Ward Beecher. Because of inflation, I updated it by changing the monetary amounts in his story.

"A nervous young man applied for a job in a New England factory. He asked for the owner, and the man asked him the reason for his coming. He shared that he was looking for work.

"'The only job here,' the owner told the applicant, 'is a vice-presidency. The man that accepts this job must shoulder all of my cares.'

"'That's a tough job,' the applicant replied. 'What is the salary?'

"The executive responded, 'I will pay you $100,000 a year if you really take over all of my worries.'

"The young man pondered the offer before questioning, 'Where is the $100,000 coming from?'

"'That, my friend,' admitted the owner, 'is your first worry'."

The second story is about a Chicago policeman who started to write a ticket for a car that had double-parked.

A man came racing out of a nearby dentist's office. He explained that he always double-parks when he visits his dentist explaining that, this way, he has something else to worry about while the dentist works on him.

"Meeeeeeoooooooowwwwww!" Sounds like Sammy-itis to me.

CHAPTER THIRTEEN

A WALK DOWN MEMORY LANE

Judy Neuman

When I was in fifth grade, Indian arrowheads still could be found throughout the woods near Ritter Spring. The clear, bubbling water of this spring near Springfield, Missouri, provided sustenance for the Cherokee Indians who camped there many years ago on their journey from Georgia to Oklahoma. This forced exodus from their homes was called, "The Trail of Tears."

The woods were located behind Ritter Elementary School which I attended during fifth and sixth grades. My friend, Karen, and I spent many hours exploring the area. We collected arrowheads, two of which I still keep in our curio cabinet. We also gathered watercress plants near the spring to make delicious salads.

But the Cherokees had moved on long before we discovered this special place. Ritter Spring was only a temporary home for them.

During the Great Depression, a transient camp was built by the stream, consisting of several simple cabins for the downtrodden. Karen and I loved to rummage through these abandoned dwellings, finding only pieces of discarded newspapers and clothing.

But that camp also had provided temporary housing. The residents had left, hoping for a better life somewhere else.

SILVER, ANYONE?

Bob and I love to sightsee in beautiful Colorado. We believe in the omnipresence of God, which means that He is present everywhere. In spite of that, each time we vacation in Colorado, we enjoy listening to a song that states, "If God doesn't live in Colorado, I bet that's where He spends most of His time."

It is fun to drive by the old ghost towns. One abandoned mining town still has many homes left standing, and upon first glance, it looks like any other town. Then it becomes obvious that there is no visible life there, no playing children, no cars driving down the streets, and no place left to shop for supplies.

This had been a temporary home for the miners as long as there was silver in "them thar hills."

THE LIGHTS ARE ON
BUT NOBODY'S HOME!

Several years ago, my widowed father was planning to re-marry, so he and his bride decided to sell their individual homes, and invest in a new one together.

Since I had spent most of my high school and college years living in that aged, remodeled farmhouse, the selling of it was a sad experience for me.

While in Missouri for a visit, Bob and I drove to the empty home and, as he waited in the car, I took one last walk through the house. Wonderful memories flooded my mind of family dinners around the table in our sunny kitchen.

After my brother, Steve, and I moved out of the house, Dad knocked out the wall between my bedroom (which later became Steve's room) and the kitchen, greatly enlarging the tiny eating area. We joked about the removal of that bedroom being their clever method of keeping us from moving back home.

I took one last look in the bathroom mirror where, during high school, I had styled and restyled my hair before going on dates. On icy winter mornings, I warmed my bones by the living room fireplace before getting ready for school, thanks to Dad who always built the fire!

There were memories of many summer nights when I would climb up on our roof and watch the bright stars in the dark country sky. Then I said farewell to the old barn, which still had my initials written in chalk on the rafters.

After my walk down memory lane, I smiled to myself knowing that I had moved on to a different place in my life.

I got into the car, and Bob and I drove away.

The old farmhouse was only a temporary home, providing lodging for my wonderful family during a certain period in our lives.

But life goes on. What seems so permanent now will be but a memory in a few years. Some of the people upon whom we are dependent today may not be alive in those tomorrows. Homes and belongings can be taken away suddenly by fire, floods, tornadoes, or financial loss. It is possible that our health may deteriorate due to illness or injury. Even our relationships with people may change.

What a bleak picture I'm painting of life! Is everything as temporary as it seems?

The good news, according to the Bible, is that there is permanence to be found.

EXACTLY HOW LONG IS FOREVER?

Here are some interesting biblical facts for you to ponder.

- **God is eternal**. He has no beginning, and there is no end to His existence. That's difficult for us to comprehend, isn't it? Hear the words from Psalm 90:2, *"Before the mountains were born or You gave birth to the earth and the world, even from everlasting to everlasting, You are God."*

- **God's Word, the Bible, is eternal**. Isaiah 40:8 proclaims, *"The grass withers, the flower fades, but the word of our God stands forever."* All that He says is true, forever!

God's only begotten Son, Jesus, is eternal. *"In the beginning was the Word, and the Word was with God, and the Word was God. He was in the beginning with God"* is the testimony found in John 1:1-2.

The presence of Jesus is enduring in the lives of those who have come to Him for salvation. He assures us in the latter part of Matthew 28:20, *". . . and lo, I am with you always, even to the end of the age."*

We can have our sins removed forever by putting our trust in Jesus. Psalm 103:12 informs us that, *"As far as the east is from the west, so far has He removed our transgressions from us."* How does this happen? 1 John 1:9 answers our question, *"If we confess our sins, He is faithful and righteous to forgive us our sins and to cleanse us from all unrighteousness."*

With Jesus Christ as Master of our lives, we can have permanent relationships with other Christians. We can't even be separated by death! We will see them again in heaven!

We'll soon have a permanent home with God. Jesus declared, *"In my Father's house are many rooms; if that were not so, I would have told you, because I am going there to prepare a place for you. And if I go and prepare a place for you, I am coming again and will take you to Myself, so that where I am, there you also will be"* (John 14:2-3).

- **Another permanent home has been prepared for all who do not choose Jesus**. That place is called "hell." No one has to go there. We all have a choice. We read about those who do not know God and do not obey our Lord Jesus, *"These will pay the penalty of eternal destruction, away from the presence of the Lord and from the glory of His power"* (2 Thessalonians 1:9).

But thanks to God's merciful provision, I plan to enjoy living forever in my permanent dwelling with Him in heaven. There will be no more temporary homes for me!

BOB'S FINAL THOUGHTS

A little boy opened the big family Bible. He was fascinated as he fingered through the old pages of the sacred book. Suddenly, something fell out of the Bible.

As he bent down to pick it up, he saw that it was an old leaf that had been pressed between the pages of the Bible. Excitedly, he called out to his mother, "Momma, look what I found!" as he held up the leaf.

"What is it?" the mother asked.

With astonishment in his voice, the lad exclaimed, "I think it's Adam's underwear!"

CHAPTER FOURTEEN

OFF AND RUNNING
Bob Neuman

There probably never was a greater mismatch of two runners in the history of sports.

Contestant number one was noted for his speed, being fleet of foot, and a real professional!

Runner number two was proverbially as "slow as molasses." Perhaps the only good quality of this roly-poly, overweight fellow, was his tough skin that enabled him to ward off the mocking and jeering of others, especially that of his rival in this long-distance race.

The day of the race came, and the contestants approached the starting line. The pistol sounded and, sure enough, contestant number one soon gained a huge lead.

In fact, his lead was so great that he decided to sit down and rest for a little while. In the warmth of the sun, contestant number one actually dozed off.

As the speedster slept away, perhaps even dreaming of standing in the winner's circle, contestant number two overtook him, crossed the finish line, and won the race!

What is incredible is that this really happened.

Well . . . sort of. All of us as children accepted this as being a real race between two runners. By now you've probably guessed that I'm talking about "The Tortoise and the Hare."

FROM A BUNNY TO THE BUCKEYES

A Bowl game in January, 2007, would determine the national championship for collegiate football, as two teams with identical records of 13 wins and only one loss faced each other in Glendale, Arizona. The Ohio State "Buckeyes" would challenge the Florida "Gators."

Just like the tortoise, the Florida Gators were the underdogs ("undergators?"). Ohio State was favored to win the game by one touchdown, and that's how the game began, but only for an instant.

On the opening kickoff, Ted Ginn, Jr., returned the pigskin for 93-yards and six points. The extra point gave the Buckeyes a very early 7-0 lead!

However, a few minutes later, Ginn hobbled off the field with a foot injury after Ohio State's first offensive play from the line of scrimmage. By the time Ginn returned for the second half on crutches, his Buckeyes were down 34-14, and the Gators would run away with college football's national title by a final score of 41-14.

After the game, Jim Tressel, the Buckeyes' coach, summarized it in these few words: "Ohio State didn't get it done."

OH, NO! NOT AGAIN!

I've been a Chicago sports fan for all of my life, so I was ecstatic when I knew that it wasn't a dream. The Chicago Bears were going to the 2006 season's "big game," the Super Bowl. It was Super Bowl XLI (that's "41" for you non-Roman folks) to be played before a sold-out crowd at Dolphin Stadium in rainy Miami, Florida.

Once again, just like the rabbit in my first illustration, and Ted Ginn Jr., in the second one, it appeared that the Bears would upset their rivals, the Indianapolis Colts. There was one difference between this football illustration and the previous one, because the Bears were one-touchdown underdogs ("underbears?") in this contest.

Sure enough, for Chicago fans, it would be a case of *déjà vu* . . . or *"déjà vu all over again,"* as the late Yogi Berra would refer to such things. By the way, *"déjà vu"* is French for "already seen," and means "The feeling that one has had an experience previously, although it is actually new." What most people don't know, and what we Chicago sports fans, especially Cubs fans know, is that *"déjà vu"* really means, "wait until next year!" [Editorial note:

Those words, "wait 'til next year," were the mantra of Cubs fans. How often we heard our enemies taunt us with, "Anyone can have a bad year. The Cubs have a bad century." Those words were finally put to rest in 2016, when the Cubs, after 108 years, finally won the World Series.]

The Colts ran roughshod over the Bears, and the game ended with a final score of 29-17.

Meanwhile, Peyton Manning, quarterback of the victorious Colts, shared, "We want to be a better team next year. We won't be taking it easy because we've won once. . . . My goal next year is to be a better quarterback, and our goal is to try and win another one. If we don't, it will be disappointing." [Another editorial note: Peyton and the Colts were disappointed, since Super Bowl 42 was won by the New York Giants, who defeated the New England Patriots by a score of 17-14.]

THE BUNNY, THE BUCKEYES, AND THE BEARS

So what do the bunny, the Buckeyes and the Bears have in common?

To quote a famous fictional detective, "It's elementary, my dear Watson."

Each of them started well, but did not finish well.

The Buckeyes and the Bears celebrated in the end zone after their opening kickoff returns. However, to change the analogy, country singer Kenny Rogers reminded us, "You never count your money (in a card game) while sitting at the table. There'll be time enough for counting, when the dealing's done."

Unfortunately, the final count of 14 for the Buckeyes, and 17 for the Bears wasn't enough!

THE MORAL OF THE STORY

The moral, simply stated, is "Don't just start well. Finish well!"

The Apostle Paul in the Bible was probably a sports fan. He wrote a letter to the church in Corinth, which is located in Greece, the birthplace of the Olympics. Listen to his words:

"Do you not know that those who run in a race all run, but only one receives the prize? Run in such a way that you may run to win. Everyone who competes in the games exercises self-control in all things. They then do it to receive a perishable wreath, but we an imperishable. Therefore, I run in such a way, as not without aim; I box in such a way, as not beating the air; but I discipline my body and make it my slave, so that, after I have preached to others, I myself will not be disqualified" (1 Corinthians 9:24-27).

BOTH MEN KNEW THIS TRUTH

Both Jesus and the Apostle Paul knew of people who began well but finished poorly.

Worse yet, some didn't finish at all. When the teaching of Jesus became more to the point, we read, *"As a result of this many of His disciples withdrew and were not walking with Him anymore. So Jesus said to the twelve, 'You do not want to go away also, do you?' Simon Peter answered Him, 'Lord, to whom shall we go? You have the words of eternal life'."* (John 6:66-69).

In a letter that Paul wrote to the believers at the church in Galatia, he noted that some false teachers had entered the church fellowship, and their false doctrines were leading the young Christians away from the truth of God's free gift of grace (undeserved favor). He asked them this question, *"You were running well; who hindered you from obeying the truth?"* (Galatians 5:7).

How are *you* progressing in the spiritual race of life?

BOB'S FINAL THOUGHTS

The year was 2007. Our younger daughter, Lori, was finishing her two-year course of study to become a dental hygienist. The class recently had a school photograph taken. I suggested that they should have worn the gruesome-looking plastic teeth that are popular around Halloween. When told to "Smile," they would flash their horrible, discolored toothy smiles. Underneath the photo could be the caption:

Prairie State College—

Dental Hygienists

Class of 2007!

What a way to finish the course!

CHAPTER FIFTEEN

ZZZZZAPPED!

Judy Neuman

It was my first radiation treatment for breast cancer in 2011, and my nerves were a little "jangled!" However, everything went like clockwork, until I heard these words:

"Mrs. Neuman, you may **not** wash your upper left torso, including your underarm, for the five-and-a-half-weeks of treatment. You may use plain water, but no soap, lotion, powder, or deodorant."

I was aghast at this new revelation. Before that, I hadn't realized that **shock treatment** was included with my radiation treatment. And, I was indeed in shock.

My calm, controlled response was, **"WHAT?"**

I could picture myself arriving for my final treatment at the end of several "undeodorized" weeks:

The technician: "Mrs. Neuman, are you ready for your last treatment?"

Me: "I'm 'game' . . . and a little 'gamey'!"

TO BE FOREWARNED
IS TO BE FOREARMED

A note to my friends and acquaintances: "Don't be offended if I stand sideways while we're talking. I'm just trying to aim my deodorized side toward you."

I was told that I could use baking soda or corn starch on my armpit. Anything is better than nothing! My husband, Bob, wondered how long he should leave me in the oven.

"YUCK" . . . THAT IS SPELLED "PEW-WEE!"

All of us hate to feel, or smell, dirty! Just think how much of our hard-earned money is spent on soaps, lotions, and deodorants per year! Most of those are scented.

I could shower with apricot soap, smooth on vanilla body butter, top it off with Old Spice deodorant, and have an apple-cinnamon candle burning on the bathroom sink. The family would think that lunch was ready. Is anybody hungry?

WHAT A CONTRAST

What a blessing it is to feel clean! When our girls were teenagers, our shower was going constantly. (Bob said that maybe I should mention that we also used the shower.)

We are all so careful to cleanse our bodies; but what about our inner persons, our souls, our spirits?

During the earthly ministry of Jesus Christ, He encountered many Jewish religious leaders who meticulously followed ceremonial rituals of washing themselves. In their minds, these procedures contributed to their inner cleansing and made them "holy."

Jesus very bluntly, but truthfully, called them "hypocrites," and quoted the prophet Isaiah saying, *"This people honors Me with their lips, but their heart is far away from Me. But in vain do they worship Me, teaching as doctrines the precepts of men"* (Matthew 15:8-9).

Then He explained, *"For out of the heart come evil thoughts, murders, adulteries, fornications, thefts, false witness, slanders. These are the things which defile a man; but to eat with unwashed hands does not defile the man"* (Matthew 15:19-20).

So, according to Jesus, all the water in the world could not make our inner selves clean. We are inclined to think evil thoughts, say evil things, or act in an evil manner. Our attitudes and motives are not always good. The Bible calls this "sin."

IT'S TIME FOR ALL OF US TO "COME CLEAN"

We need to have our sins "cleaned out" of our hearts. These sins will eventually destroy our relationships with people, as well as with God.

Long before He created our world, God had a plan that would allow us to be forgiven for our sins. He would send His only Son, Jesus Christ, to this sin-infested world to die on the cross.

Though Jesus was completely innocent, He took our punishment upon Himself! What love He demonstrated for us!

It is only because of the blood that flowed from His body that we can be set free from the chains of sin that bind us! The following hymn says it so well:

<u>*Nothing but the Blood*</u>

What can wash away my sin?

Nothing but the blood of Jesus;

What can make me whole again?

Nothing but the blood of Jesus.

For my pardon this I see

Nothing but the blood of Jesus;

For my cleansing this my plea

Nothing but the blood of Jesus.

Oh! Precious is the flow

That makes me white as snow;

No other fount I know,

Nothing but the blood of Jesus.

The promise in First John 1:9 is, *"If we confess our sins, He is faithful and righteous to forgive us our sins and to cleanse us from all unrighteousness."*

As soon as my radiation treatments were completed, I was able to cleanse my body the old-fashioned way, using my trusty bar of Lever soap. I was so thankful when that day arrived (and so was Bob.)

However, I have to admit that I am much more thankful for a clean heart.

BOB'S FINAL THOUGHTS

I had two suggestions for Judy during her treatments.

First, I said that she should ask people this question, "Would you like to stand next to my 'Right Guard' side or my 'Left Unguarded' side?"

My second suggestion was that she stay downwind of other people.

What a helpful husband I am!

CHAPTER SIXTEEN

AN OLD DOG GETS A NEW BONE

Bob Neuman

Let me begin with a confession. As a pastor, I know that whenever a clergyman utters the phrase, "I have a confession to make," he has everybody's attention.

When it comes to computers, I'm from the "old school." I started out with a large writing tablet, and a sharpened Number 2 pencil. Remember those?

One day, I graduated to an Etch-a-Sketch!

I remember the day that I finally bought my first computer. I did so without seeking anybody's advice. I later read a statement, attributed to Abraham Lincoln, that declares, "He who represents himself has a fool for a client."

Why, hello Bob!

The computer was purchased years ago from the owner of an office supply store in Lansing, Illinois. The store is no longer in business. Maybe that was prophetic.

The machine was not quite as large as Manhattan Island. It just seemed that way. It had a small amount of memory (like the man who purchased it), and operated on the Windows system. I think it was Windows One. The word-processing program was so obsolete that I still joke about buying a copy of the antiquated word processing software for my son-in-law, Tim, for Christmas!

Over the course of years, Earl, a deacon in our church and an AT&T employee, refurbished two laptops for me. But in Indianapolis, on a church-related trip, I turned on my old laptop, and was dismayed to see that the picture just rolled and rolled.

Being the wise man, or wise guy, that I am, I quickly discovered that there was no horizontal hold button on the back of the machine. I eventually was able to "tame" it, but decided that it was time to take the next step.

I decided not to represent myself in buying a laptop, so I called upon my son-in-law, Tim.

IT WAS TIME TO MODERNIZE!

Tim is the kind of guy who has forgotten more about computers than I ever learned. I called and shared with Tim that I was thinking about buying a new laptop, and needed his advice. He told me he would check on some prices, and get back in touch with me. This article could be called, "Bob and Tim's Great Adventure!"

True to his word, Tim called and suggested we meet at a local Best Buy. We arrived at the store almost simultaneously. Tim strode confidently into the store, and I puffed out my chest and followed, exerting all the pseudo-confidence I could muster.

As we entered the store, Tim headed directly to the section that sold "all things computer." I was glad that I did not go by myself, for I would have been like Moses and the children of Israel. Forty years later I would have found the Promised Land of Laptops!

WHERE'S HENRY?

The store had so many laptops on display that they could have covered the national debt! I thought of the early days of the Ford automobile, and Henry Ford who declared, "You can have this car in any color, as long as it is black," and wished for those simpler days in "Laptopville."

Tim moved briskly among the rows of laptops, flitting from one to another like a bee searching for just the right pollen-laden flower.

He paused and began to tell me about some of the features of each one, using words like "processor," "hard drive," "wireless," "rewrite capacity," etc. Whenever he starts talking like that, Natalie, our older daughter, who is Tim's wife, looks at Tim. Then she quips, "Tim, Dad's eyes just glazed over!" On that day I'm sure they glazed over so much that I could have been the poster boy for Dunkin' Donuts' "Glazed-Donut-Eyes-Man," if they ever needed one!

I moved to a higher-priced laptop, and asked Tim about it. He began speaking in the foreign language of "computerese," and all I remember were his final words in English which were, "You don't need all those bells and whistles." I'm sure he said that because he knew that, if I had purchased that particular model, I would be calling him later asking him, "Tim, how do I turn on the bells?" Or, perhaps, even query, "When it comes to the whistles, am I to blow out or suck in?"

Tim decided on the laptop just as a young saleslady approached. It was then that the interrogation began. Aware that I was probably the buyer, she asked **me** a question.

Helplessly and hopelessly, I looked at Tim with my usual clueless expression, and he quickly answered her question. Confidently, I "parroted" his words. She probably thought that I did not speak English and, when it comes to computers, I'm not sure that I do!

Then she asked about "opening" the computer, and doing something with the programs, or something like that, adding the words, "for an extra fee."

Tim picked up on her question and responded, "No. That's why he has his son-in-law!" (Can you see why I love this guy?)

HOLD IT, CHARLIE! WE'RE NOT DONE YET!

The saleslady excused herself to see if Best Buy had our selection in stock. Tim said, "Now, we need a router."

After hearing Tim talk about "hardware" and "software," I'm glad he did not suggest that I buy a router later by myself. Here is the hypothetical scenario:

Tim: "Bob, did you buy a router?"

Bob, (responding with great confidence): "Yes, Tim, I did."

Tim: "Where did you buy it?"

Bob: "I bought it at Ace Hardware."

Tim (looking at me and wondering how I could have been the father of such a brilliant daughter): "Oh, Bob. I'm so sorry. You bought a router for woodworking. What you need is a wireless router for your laptop."

Perhaps fearful that the above dialogue might really happen, Tim announced, "I'll pick up a router and bring it by your house."

"ALL SYSTEMS GO!"

The next day, Tim stopped by my house to get everything connected. Do you remember how I told you Tim had flitted around at Best Buy? Well, when he arrived at my house, he either acted more like a bee with Attention-Deficit/Hyperactivity Disorder (ADHD), or an insect on adrenalin high!

He connected and disconnected wires from my desktop, hooked up wires to the wireless router, and entered a password. His actions reminded me of the words that caused me to sit on the edge of my seat. The announcer began, "A fiery horse with the speed of light, a cloud of dust, and a hearty 'Hi-Yo Silver,' . . . The Lone Ranger!" It seemed to me as if Tim opened and closed Windows so fast it made my head spin. Then Tim "folded his tent like the Arab" and silently stole away.

"HOUSTON, WE HAVE A PROBLEM!"

The next day, I set the new laptop on the kitchen counter and attempted several times to connect to the Internet. So it was time for another "S.O.S. . . . Mayday! . . . Help!" cry from me to Tim.

Noticing on his caller identification that it was me, he answered in a phony foreign accent, "Tech support." I explained to Tim the problem I was having. Once again, he promised to stop by after work to trouble shoot the problem. I'm sure he would have been happier trouble shooting the owner!

That evening, he did a diagnostic test and thought I needed a better router, so he promised to buy one and return later. When he did so, he discovered that the cheaper one was just as good. He said, "Bob, the problem is that the computer and the router are talking with each other, but are not reading each other's signals," and . . . yes, my eyes did glaze over!

Then he showed me why I could not get the wireless signal, and even created a shortcut for me. Eventually, he solved the problem, no doubt thinking, "Next time, **do not** call Tim!"

V IS FOR VICTORY!

I have three nicknames for my wonderful, technologically-minded, son-in-law. Sometimes I call him, "The Timster." At other times I have dubbed him, "The Tim Man." But, because he is able to teach an old dog like me new tricks, my favorite moniker for him is, "The Boy Wonder!"

BOB'S FINAL THOUGHTS

All of us need help in life at one time or another. I'm glad God is always there, but that, in His providence, He sent me a tremendously helpful son-in-law. Galatians 6:2 instructs us, *"Bear one another's burdens, and thereby fulfill the law of Christ."*

CHAPTER SEVENTEEN

THE BIRDS AND THE BEES—RATED PG!

Judy Neuman

"Do you know about the birds and the bees?" Those words were the beginning of a conversation I overheard years ago between our three-year-old daughter, Natalie, and her slightly-older playmate, Tammy.

Natalie confidently replied to Tammy's question by saying, "Yes, I do! The birds tweet, and the bees buzz."

It was obvious that Bob and I had not yet had "the talk" with Natalie about procreation.

LIKE MOTHER, LIKE DAUGHTER

In some families, parents postpone this delicate discussion until the children start asking questions. That plan did not work very well between my parents and me.

I was too shy to ask questions. (My, how my personality has changed over time. Now it's difficult to keep me quiet!)

Finally, Mom just gave me a book that explained everything I needed to know, and I read it from cover to cover. Bob joked that, as a matter of fact, we took that book on our honeymoon.

FAST FORWARD SEVERAL YEARS

When true love finally captured my heart, I was still a little naïve. It's a good thing Bob didn't ask me if I knew about the birds and the bees. I probably would have said, "Yes, I do! The birds tweet and the bees buzz!"

Bob quips that he probably would have thought that I had given him the correct answer.

Bob proposed to me only one-and-one-half months after our first date. We still celebrate the anniversary of that first date every year by returning to Steak 'n Shake, the restaurant chain at which we frequently ate on our dates. We believed that no expense was too great for true love.

One year later, we were married and, "The rest is history."

TO SPEAK OR NOT TO SPEAK?

When Bob proposed to me, he said, "Judy, I think I love you." He was very hesitant to speak, and was afraid I would not return his affection.

However, I answered in like manner, "Bob, I think I love you, too."

As you can see, confidence was not our greatest quality in those days.

Fast forward over a half-century to the present. Those "I think" words resulted in a great marriage, two wonderful daughters, Natalie and Lori, and an amazing son-in-law, Tim. God has truly blessed us.

LOOKING BACK IN REVIEW

Were our many years of marriage always a bed of roses? Of course not! Even roses have thorns, bees sting, and birds lose their tweets.

When our long-time friends, Harold and Pearl, were celebrating their 50th wedding anniversary, Pearl said to us, "In all these years, we never considered divorce. Murder, yes; divorce no!"

The secret to our long, happy marriage is the fact that Bob and I are traveling through life in the same direction. (He adds that many times he has to stop, and ask me which way we're going.)

Long before we met, we each surrendered our life to God. In our marriage, we learned to yield to His guidance along the path of life. God openly reveals His plans for living in His holy Word, the Bible.

LOOK INTO THE WORD

Many of you memorized the 23rd Psalm. But have you accepted it as your personal testimony? It begins, *"The Lord is my shepherd."* That's personal . . . my shepherd!

Most of my memorization of scripture was from the King James Version of the Bible that was widely used during my childhood. But this paraphrase from *The Living Bible* is also special to me.

PSALM 23

1. Because the Lord is my Shepherd, I have everything I need!

2. *He lets me rest in the meadow grass and leads me beside the quiet streams.*

3. *He restores my failing health. He helps me do what honors him the most.*

4. *Even when walking through the dark valley of death, I will not be afraid, for you are close beside me, guarding all the way.*

5. *You provide delicious food for me in the presence of my enemies. You have welcomed me as your guest; blessings overflow!*

When a husband and wife agree on whom the Shepherd is, which road to travel, the direction of travel, and the destination, life together is as fulfilling as life can possibly be! Bob and I are living proof of that fact.

Jesus said, *"I am the Good Shepherd. The Good Shepherd lays down his life for the sheep"* (John 10:11). And Jesus did give His life for us, His sheep.

If you surrender your life to Jesus, the Good Shepherd, then you belong to Him. He said, *"My sheep listen to my voice, and I know them, and they follow me. I give them eternal life and they shall never perish...."* (John 10:27-28).

The love story that Bob and I share is very special to us, but the greatest love story is this: *"But God demonstrates his own love for us in this: While we were still sinners, Christ died for us"* (Romans 5:8).

BOB'S FINAL THOUGHTS

Several years ago, I read a true story about a farmer who had gone to a big city department store. It was shortly before Valentine's Day, and it was crowded, as many men were looking for just the right gift for their wife or sweetheart.

He decided to buy a new nightgown for his wife. As he was looking over the various choices, he noticed a young, professional businessman approach the clerk. He was holding a lovely, black, lacy gown. The man purchased the item, and the clerk wrapped it in a beautiful box, placing a ribbon on it.

The old farmer approached the clerk. He pointed toward the young man who had just bought the nightgown. Sheepishly, he asked, "Would you happen to have anything in black flannel?"

CHAPTER EIGHTEEN

APPEARANCES CAN BE DECEIVING

Judy Neuman

It was the mid 1930s, and a hearse proceeded down the two-lane highway from Salamanca, New York, to Cherry Creek, New York.

People watched respectfully as it drove by, perhaps breathing out prayers for the grieving family. When the hearse was manufactured in 1925, it was "top of the line" with its wooden seats (ouch!), and running boards along the sides.

But, wait a minute! There was no dead body inside the hearse. Instead, it transported a family of eight kids, and two or three adults on their way to a family reunion 35 miles away. I can picture it now: kids laughing, arms hanging out of the windows, bodies, (live ones at that) competing for the window seats.

Our late friend, Jeannine, related this story to us, and revealed that her Uncle Orin worked for an auto dealership that rented out the hearse to funeral homes. Since Jeannine's family did not own a car at the time, Uncle Orin chauffeured their large family to the reunion in that luxury vehicle.

Things are not always as they seem!

BARNEY FIFE, PERHAPS?

Several years ago, Bob and I drove from our home in Calumet City, Illinois, to a vacation place in Frazier, Colorado. We drove across Wyoming and, at Laramie, headed south towards Colorado.

As we approached a small town, we were surprised to see a police car parked in a driveway, positioned to pull onto the highway. Behind the wheel sat a uniformed policeman, no doubt eyeing us as we drove by, hoping to strike fear in our hearts.

All of a sudden, Bob laughed out loud, slowed the car, and pointed at the policeman. As I followed Bob's finger, I also began to laugh. The police car was real, but the policeman was a "dummy," a huge, stuffed doll in uniform! Those townspeople sure fooled us . . . for a while.

Things aren't always as they seem!

WAS IT A MORNING LIKE THIS?

That particular Friday morning began as an ordinary day for most of the population. People scurried here and there doing their shopping. Women worked in their kitchens, preparing food for the day. The laughter of children could be heard all over town as they played with their friends, or made their way to school.

But something was very different about that day.

Somebody was going to die!

Yes, death takes place all over the world, but this death would be different.

The man on death row did not look like a criminal. In fact, he had never been in jail before. His family and friends loved him, and believed that he had been falsely accused. However, those in authority had issued a death sentence for him.

And, as strange as it may seem, even though the man knew that he was innocent, he was at peace with his fate, and refused to defend himself.

As the hour of his execution drew near, the prisoner was almost unrecognizable. He had been so mistreated, humiliated, and beaten that his loved ones were shocked and saddened by his disfigurement.

It seemed that day that even nature itself was grieving, for as he slipped toward death, the sky grew frighteningly dark!

Several hours later, his suffering was over. He was dead. As the observers went their way, a kind, wealthy benefactor transported him to his own cemetery plot and gave him a respectful, hasty burial.

Quickly, the town settled back into its normal routine, and the dead man's loved ones began to reminisce about his short life and his unjust death.

Oh, by the way, the dead man's name was . . . Jesus!

But hadn't He claimed to be the Messiah, the anointed Son of God who would take away the sins of the world?

Now that He was dead and buried, how could this promised cleansing of sin take place? Didn't this prove that He was just an ordinary man who did some good deeds along the way, before facing death like the rest of us?

Praise God, Jesus' death is not the end of the story!

Remember . . . things are not always as they seem.

THINGS ARE DIFFERENT NOW

As the sun rose on that glorious Sunday morning, life changed for all of mankind. That includes you, me, and every person yet unborn.

Jesus arose from the grave. That cold, dark, borrowed tomb was empty.

Jesus is alive, and alive forevermore!

His resurrection is the final proof of who He claimed to be, and of what He came to do on this earth.

Before Jesus was born, an angel appeared in a dream to Joseph, His earthly father, giving specific instructions concerning the baby. He said, *". . . you shall call His name Jesus, for He will save His people from their sins"* (Matthew 1:21).

A dead, decaying body has no power to save the world.

However, the resurrected Son of God *". . . is able to save forever those who draw near to God through Him since He always lives to make intercession for them"* (Hebrews 7:25).

Later, in a vision given to the apostle John, Jesus Himself said, *". . . Do not be afraid; I am the first and the last, and the living*

One; and I was dead, and behold, I am alive forevermore, and I have the keys of death and of Hades" (Revelation 1:17-18).

BOB'S FINAL THOUGHTS

The taxi driver was transporting a man down the darkened road. Suddenly, the passenger reached over the seat and tapped the cabbie on his shoulder.

The driver let out a blood-curdling scream, slammed on the brakes, and veered the cab into the curb with a loud thud!

The shocked "fare" in the back seat apologized for startling the cab driver.

The driver explained his reaction. "You see," he began, "I'm new as a cab driver. For the last 35 years, I've driven a hearse."

Yes, things are not always as they seem. (That wasn't Uncle Orin driving the cab, was it?)

CHAPTER NINETEEN

"DO YOU KNOW THE WAY TO SAN JOSE?"
Bob Neuman

Judy and I have been blessed to be able to travel quite a bit during our married life. We have been to 47 of the 50 states, including five cruises to Alaska.

The three states remaining on our bucket list are Maine, North Dakota, and Hawaii. I have been researching for years, but still have not come up with a way to visit all three states on a road trip!

In addition to these "United States," we have been to Canada, Mexico, Israel, Greece, and Turkey. We spent 10 days in Greece to celebrate our 50th wedding anniversary.

Judy has always been the navigator on our trips. I thought of the lyrics from the hymn by Edward Hopper that declares, "Chart and compass come from Thee. Jesus, Saviour, pilot me."

In the first several years of our travels, Judy packed enough maps to wallpaper the state of Rhode Island.

We loaded the car, headed off to "parts known," while crooning along with Willie Nelson, "On the Road Again." Very seldom did we have to stop and ask for directions. This is the scourge of most men. Those instances were usually because of encountering a detour, or needing specific directions to a restaurant.

"WE'VE BEEN EVERYWHERE, MAN!"

Let me add a "disclaimer" to the above heading. It's not really true. We have had the privilege of visiting the Badlands of South Dakota and Devil's Tower in Wyoming, but were unable to convert either of them.

We enjoyed Mt. Rushmore, and witnessed the four stone-carved U. S. Presidents looking down their noses at us from their lofty perch. How disrespectful!

We watched as the Crazy Horse memorial was being carved out of another mountain. Please do not confuse Crazy Horse with "Charlie horse," the malady that often strikes one's leg in the middle of the night!

And, who, might I ask, has ever visited South Dakota without stopping at Wall Drug, if for no other reason than for the promised glass of ice-cold water?

We've seen the large group of Harley Davidson bikers from across the nation on their annual migration to Sturgis, South Dakota. They reminded us of salmon returning to their spawning grounds.

Judy and I even "popped in" to see the Corn Palace in Mitchell, South Dakota.

We have never been to Stonehenge in England. However, one day, as we were traveling through Nebraska, we saw a quirky attraction called Carhenge, an artistic compilation of automobiles in Stonehenge formation. It so perfectly replicates the real Stonehenge that the summer solstice even happens there in the same manner as it does in England.

Our travels have taken us to many historic places, such as Plymouth Rock, Arlington National Cemetery, Ft. McHenry, the Statue of Liberty, and the Everglades.

We watched as the mighty waters cascaded over Niagara Falls, and witnessed the sun work its artistic handiwork on the beautiful Painted Desert, and saw the sun set on the Golden Gate Bridge.

Judy and I have visited over 25% of the 59 national parks in the United States, including Denali in Alaska. But, no, we haven't been everywhere yet!

We marveled as we watched Old Faithful in Yellowstone National Park erupt on schedule, as it spewed its steamy mist high into the air.

As we stood on the edge of the Grand Canyon, or in Glacier National Park, we could not help but think of the great hymn that declared, "How Great Thou Art."

"A BRIDGE OVER TROUBLED WATERS"

Judy and I were vacationing in Colorado several years ago. While there, we learned that Avon, Colorado., erected a new bridge. It was a 150-foot four-lane structure that spanned the Eagle River.

The Avon Town Council held a contest to choose an official name for the bridge. The bridge was named, "Bob," by a 4-to-2 vote of the Council.

One of the Council members that voted against naming the bridge, "Bob," was Councilwoman Gloria McRory. She said that naming the bridge, "Bob," made light of all the work required to coordinate the state, the county, and the railroad. She wanted something more serious, "Ernest," perhaps.

Ed Quillen wrote in the Oct. 30, 1991, issue of *The Denver Post*, "My nomination would be literary. William Shakespeare hailed from Stratford *on* Avon. If 'Bob' were named 'Stratford,' then Colorado could boast a 'Stratford *on* Avon,' and we might attract a few stupid tourists...."

Speaking of "stupid tourists," one Saturday morning, Judy and I drove several miles to Avon. It was raining heavily as I disembarked from the car, and stood by the sign next to the bridge that read, "Bob," while Judy snapped a picture as water dripped from my face.

I wondered why Ed Quillen would write about "stupid tourists."

"PLEASE DON'T SQUEEZE THE 'GARMIN'!"

We eventually upgraded from a bushel bag full of road maps to a small device called a Garmin GPS, which we nicknamed, "Bubbette."

In 2012, Judy, "Bubbette," and I flew from Chicago, Illinois, to Boston, Massachusettts, where we took a senior citizen cruise organized by our church's national headquarters.

We visited Halifax, Nova Scotia, and St. John, New Brunswick. I had met Geoffe Clark, a pastor from St. John, on the Internet. When he and his wife, Hazel, learned our ship would be in St. John, they volunteered to be our gracious hosts for a few hours.

They drove us to the Bay of Fundy, and we ate at Tim Horton's. They demonstrated great northern hospitality, and treated us royally.

When we returned to Boston, we rented a car to drive to Philadelphia, Pennsylvania, and Delaware. As we started out on our journey, Judy turned on the Garmin, which said we were 750 miles from Philadelphia.

I may be a "stupid tourist," but it sure didn't look like "Beantown" and "The city of brotherly love" were that far apart on a regular map. It was then that Judy discovered that she had failed to inform "Bubbette" that our "starting point" was not our home in Illinois!

Instead of driving back to Illinois, she entered "Boston" as our starting point. We rejoiced that we were just a little more than 300 miles from Philadelphia, and Judy entered the new coordinates into the Garmin.

Later, we purchased a newer Garmin that we named "Bubbacita." However, "she" started suffering from what I diagnosed as D. D. S. (Directional Dysfunctional Syndrome).

The following week, Judy called a customer service representative with the company who urged her to upgrade the software, which we did.

It was not long after we upgraded the software on the Garmin that we attended an interleague Major League Baseball game between the Northside Chicago Cubs, and the Southside Chicago White Sox. Each summer, this inner-city rivalry is called "The Crosstown Classic." That day's game was to be played at the beautiful confines of Wrigley Field.

Chicago was celebrating its annual "Taste of Chicago" festival. Because this huge event causes major traffic jams along Chicago's lakefront, Judy and I decided to go a different route, relying upon "Bubbacita" to guide us.

However, our software problem obviously was more serious. The unit would shut off automatically. Judy would unplug it for a few minutes, and then restart the unit.

Our problems continued unabated, so later Judy again called customer service, believing that "It's the squeaky wheel that gets the oil." After explaining our dilemma, she was told to return the Garmin and the company would send us a free replacement.

"Free" is our favorite word.

ALL ROADS DO NOT LEAD TO ROME!

Not every road will get us to our desired eternal destination of heaven.

The road marked, "good works," won't do it.

Neither will the highway of, "moral living."

Yes, even just believing that "church membership" itself will guarantee our arrival there may prove fatal!

Jesus said, *"I am the way, and the truth, and the life; no one comes to the Father but through Me."*

I don't need a Garmin to tell me what I need to do. I simply need to accept God's truth, believe it, and confess my sins.

Believe me, heaven will be unlike any earthly destination anyone can imagine!

TWO FINAL THOUGHTS

First, when our Garmin replacement arrived, according to tradition, we named it.

We chose the name, "Bubba Sue," and we are praying that life will be easy "for a GPS named Bubba Sue!"

Second, after I first wrote this article, I came across something clever about travel that somebody posted on the Internet. After all, you can believe everything you see on the Internet. It read:

"I have been in many places, but I've never been in Cahoots. Apparently, you can't go alone. You have to be in Cahoots with someone.

"I've also never been in Cognito. I hear no one recognizes you there.

"I have, however, been in Sane. They don't have an airport; you have to be driven there. I have made several trips there, thanks to my friends, family and work. I live close so it's a short drive.

"I would like to go to Conclusions, but you have to jump, and I'm not too much on jumping any more.

"I have also been in Doubt. That is a sad place to go, and I try not to visit there too often.

"I've been in Flexible, but only when it was very important to stand firm.

Sometimes I'm in Capable, and I go there more often as I'm getting older.

"One of my favorite places to be is in Suspense! It really gets the adrenalin flowing and pumps up the old heart! At my age, I need all the stimuli I can get!

"And, sometimes I think I am in Vincible, but life shows me I am not.

"People keep telling me I'm in Denial, but I'm positive I've never been there before.

"So far, I haven't been in Continent. But my urologist says I'll be going soon."

CHAPTER TWENTY

IT WASN'T
THAT KIND OF WEDDING
Bob Neuman

This chapter is NOT about MY big fat Greek wedding for the following reasons:

First, I am not Greek. I leave it to those who know me personally to decide if the adjectives "big" and "fat" apply. But, please . . . be kind!

Second, I would not want to rip off Nia Vardalos, the creative writer and star of the hit independent film, and the CBS television program, *My Big Fat Greek Wedding*.

Third, I choose not to expose myself to possible litigation from Warner Home Video, CBS, Ms. Vardalos, etc.

O.K., friends, I did learn my lesson from Jayson Blair!

Jayson who?

Blair was the 27-year-old former reporter for *The New York Times* who was forced to resign for engaging in fabrications, scams, and plagiarism.

Having said all of that, I invite you to sit back, relax, and enjoy the true life adventure titled:

OUR LITTLE SKINNY OZARK WEDDING

Judy and I were married on June 25, 1965, in Springfield, Missouri. Our wedding wasn't the stereotypical Ozarkian wedding, where the father of the bride, brandishing a 12-gauge shotgun, makes sure the young man does the honorable thing by marrying his daughter.

Nor was our wedding the type in which the groom and groomsmen wore ritzy tuxedoes with cumberbunds.

Nor was it a Chicago-style blue-collar wedding in which the men wore their fanciest bowling jackets with tri-colored bowling shoes.

On the other hand, it wasn't the lowliest wedding either, with the groom (me) wearing a stylish 1960s leisure suit and the groomsmen decked out in their "dress" OshKosh B'gosh bibbed overalls, covered with the remnants from last weekend's barbecue.

My accomplices in crime, er, marriage, weren't "Bubba and the boys," as one might have anticipated. My entourage consisted of Ray Ramsey, my childhood friend who served as my best man, and my late college roommate, Marvin Cavanaugh, who was my groomsman. I think they agreed to be in my wedding because I promised them cake and punch. But, hey, what are friends for, anyhow?

Do you remember the following parody of the wedding song?

Here comes the bride,

Big, fat, and wide.

Here comes the groom,

Skinny as a broom.

There's truth in that description of the groom, since I was about half the man at our wedding than I am now. Judy told me to leave out the part about the bride being "big, fat, and wide." However, I will admit that none of those adjectives applied to her, since she, too, was "skinny as a broom." Judy always reminds me of the Bible verse, "Husbands, obey your wives." She says that is what her version of the Bible says. So, who am I to argue with her?

In the interest of an opposing viewpoint, it's Judy's turn to share.

DECISIONS, DECISIONS
Judy Neuman

What an amazing coincidence that both of our weddings took place on exactly the same day, at the same time, and at the same place!

Before I share about our wedding, let me rewind those memories to a period about two years before Bob and I walked down the aisle to say, "I do."

At that time, Bob and I had not even met each other. He was preparing to attend Central Bible College in Springfield, Missouri, now a part of Evangel University, and was dating a nice girl, also named Judy, who lived close to Bob's hometown of Hammond, Indiana.

During that period, I was a student at Southwest Missouri State College (now Missouri State University) in Springfield, my birthplace. I was dating a very special young man who would drive about 40 miles each way to take me out every weekend. In the back of my mind, I thought perhaps this was "the one." He was a Christian, handsome, had been a basketball star at his high school, and treated me with great respect. We even went roller skating together, an activity which, later, I could never persuade Bob to try.

But there was still something missing. One night, as I was praying before bedtime, I sincerely committed my marital future to God, pledging that I would stay sensitive to His guidance, even if He wanted me to remain single, rather than to forge ahead on my own and possibly marry the wrong person.

OZARK MOUNTAIN "I DO'S"

A few weeks later, Audrey, a coworker at the Gospel Publishing House, played the role of a matchmaker and introduced me to a new employee named, Bob Neuman. Like Quasimodo, does that name ring a bell?

While still dating the other guy, I began to see Bob regularly, not realizing that we were falling in love. On our first date, I knew there was something different about him, besides his off-the-wall sense of humor. We seemed to be heading in the same direction spiritually, and our personalities blended perfectly.

Within a month, Bob proposed to me, and I said, "yes." Of course, this meant that both of us had to break up with our former sweethearts! Everything fell into place, and Bob and I were married a year later at Glad Tidings Assembly of God in Springfield.

Looking back, I'm so thankful that I followed God's plan. God saw the whole span of my life, and knew what was best. Bob was, and is, the right one for me! (No, folks, Bob did not write that.) We have followed the Lord throughout our years together and have allowed Jesus Christ to be the central focus of our marriage, child rearing, finances, and ministry. Our desire is to follow His footsteps daily. Of course, as humans, we have made, and will make, many mistakes in our walk with God.

Every time we send a wedding card, I write the following advice for a happy marriage.

1. Let God be central in every part of your lives.
2. Learn to "roll with the punches." There will be trials and difficulties ahead.
3. Always be best friends.
4. Laugh together every day.

When each marriage partner's life is fully surrendered to Jesus Christ, and to each other, that marriage will be strong and stable. It is His power that brings strength to that relationship. Decisions will be made based upon the principles of God's Word, the Bible, and the road ahead, no matter how treacherous, will be paved with the presence of God.

BOB'S FINAL THOUGHTS

After our vows, Judy and I were driving east on Kearney Avenue in Springfield. Our friends had taped a sign on the side of our car that read, "Watch Missouri grow!"

I stopped at a traffic light. A station wagon pulled up next to us. It was loaded with kids. As the driver politely blew his horn to get our attention, Judy rolled down her window to see what he wanted. Pointing to his children, he said, "Look! That's what happened to me!"

www.ingramcontent.com/pod-product-compliance
Lightning Source LLC
Chambersburg PA
CBHW071341150726
47997CB00002B/817